Christ in the Psalms

Brian McNeil

Christ in the Psalms

PAULIST PRESS
New York/Ramsey

Nihil obstat:
Richard Sherry, D.D.,
Censor Deputatus

Imprimatur:
+ Dermot,
Archbishop of Dublin,
April 1980

First published 1980 by Veritas Publications,
7-8 Lower Abbey Street, Dublin 1.

Published by Paulist Press
Editorial Office: 1865 Broadway, New York, N.Y. 10023
Business Office: 545 Island Road, Ramsey, N.J. 07446

Library of Congress
Catalog Card Number: 80-82796

ISBN: 0-8091-2341-X

Printed and bound in the
United States of America

To
the sisters
of the Lunden Kloster in Oslo
forenet i bönn og lovsang

ACKNOWLEDGEMENTS

The Author and the Publisher are grateful to the following for permission to reproduce copyright material in this work: A. P. Watt Ltd, London, and the Grail, England, for quotations from *The Psalms: A New Translation*, published by William Collins Sons and Co. Ltd; the National Council of the Churches of Christ in the U.S.A., New York, for quotations from the *Revised Standard Version of the Bible* (Catholic Edition) copyrighted © 1965 and 1966 by the Division of Christian Education of the National Council of the Churches of Christ in the U.S.A..

NOTE

In this book, I follow the numbering of the Psalms which is customary in Catholic liturgical books, so that, e.g., Ps 51 in the Hebrew Bible is here referred to as Ps 50. I have usually used the *Revised Standard Version* (the Common Bible) or the *Grail Psalter,* but occasionally I have given my own translation of a biblical passage; all translations of non-biblical texts are my own.

B. McN.

Contents

Introduction

This book had its origin in an invitation from Sister Anne-Lise Ström, OP, novice-mistress of the Lunden Kloster in Oslo, to give a course of talks on the prayer of the Psalms in the light of the tradition of the Church. I have preserved the basic style in which they were given in September 1979 at Lunden, and to groups at St Dominikus Kirke in Oslo and St Mary's Cathedral in Aberdeen a little later.

The book has a double aim. First, I hope it may be useful as a meditation on praying the Psalms in the fellowship of the Church. I have occasionally been asked, "Why do we pray the Psalms at all? How do they help the Christian life?" These chapters present an attempt at an answer to these fundamentally important questions; they are not a systematic theology of the prayer of the Psalms, but a series of meditations which go gradually deeper into a few significant themes. I have been convinced for a long time that the best way to learn to pray is not to read books about the theoretical side of prayer, but to do it for ourselves — if we want to discover how the prayer of the Psalms can truly become our own, the best thing to do is to begin to pray them. This is not a book to be rushed through quickly, but one which should be meditated through slowly — chewed rather than gulped!

Second, it is a book written "in the light of the tradition of the Church", and I hope that it may be useful as an introduction to the patristic readings which we have in the divine office. It does not attempt to supply any information about individual Fathers of the Church, nor to give any account of their theology and spirituality; there are other books that do that. It attempts, rather, to get to grips with the fact that when we read the Fathers in the Office of Readings, we are reading them as texts of our *prayer*. Example is so often a more powerful teacher than any volume of words can be: we read the Fathers in the office in order that they may teach us how to pray. The simplest way to find out how these texts, from cultures so alien to our own, can genuinely be a part of our daily prayer-life is to get down to the task of praying and living in the presence of God *with* the Fathers. So we shall come to know the tradition of the Church, not as a kind of exhibit we look at in a museum, but as a living process of the handing-on of life in Christ, a process which nourishes us as it nourished those who went before us. This book aims therefore to show, *by doing it,* how the spirituality of the Fathers is directly relevant for the Christians of the twentieth century. We shall try to enter into the *mind* and the *heart* of the Fathers, and make them our own, without seeking to be artificially "early-church" or thinking that we must reject all that God is saying to us in our own day.

A rediscovery of this tradition may also help our preaching. Too many of us are content to deliver a ten-minute talk on a Sunday morning about the historical background of the scripture readings of the Mass, and then to continue with the liturgy under the delusion that we have proclaimed the word of God. The historical questions (Does this saying go back to Jesus? Which king is Ezekiel talking about? What is the apocalyptic mythology all about?) are undeniably interesting; but we have to get *beyond* this stage if we are to understand what the Holy Spirit is saying to the Church today through the scriptures, and if we are to communicate that to the people of God. Much in the exegesis of the early centuries may perhaps strike us as fanciful; but, at least, it was understood that there is more to preaching than an explanation of the literal sense of the texts! We need to recover the ability to *pray* the scriptures, and I hope that this book may be a help in this.

I must express my thanks to the Sisters of the Lunden Kloster, from whom I learned a great deal about prayer in my days with them; and to Father Per-Björn Halvorsen, OP, of Oslo, and Bishop Mario Conti of Aberdeen, for their invitations to speak and the kindness of their welcome. I am indebted for much encouragement to Dr Halvor Moxnes of Oslo; to Father Gabriel Bunge, OSB, of Chevetogne; and to Professor Ernst Chr. Suttner of Vienna. And I owe a great debt to all who have aided this work by their prayers and their kindness.

Brian McNeil
Faculty of Catholic Theology
University of Vienna
4 November 1979

1 The Christian at prayer

When we speak of prayer, of man's search for God, we really must begin by speaking of God's search for us. For we love, only because he loved us first; we search, only because he searched for us first. If we have the power to look, it is only because he has planted in our hearts a seed of restlessness, an unquietness that can be stilled only in him. This strange inability to be at rest, this nagging dissatisfaction with everything in life, is, we might think, just part of the imperfectness of being human. "I have seen that all perfection has an end", says the psalmist (118:96)—words that we find coming very easily to our lips. But it is not just something human: we are made in the image and likeness of God our creator, and this continual stretching out beyond oneself is part of his divine life just as much as it is part of our human life. "All day long I have spread out my hands to a rebellious people", he says in Isaiah (65:2): he is a God who, not content to sit back and wait for the lost sheep to find its own way home, actively goes out to search for it. "I am lost like a sheep," says the psalmist (118:176), "*seek* your servant."

The whole history of our salvation is the history of this search. The unfolding of God's revelation of himself in the old covenant is the beginning of the search of God for man, of the wooing of which he speaks in Ezekiel 16. God found Israel unloved, uncared for: "No eye pitied you"; he took pity on her, and bound her to himself in an everlasting covenant. Those words of the covenant, "They shall be my people, and I will be their God", are repeated time and again in the pages of the Old Testament: they are words that attest God's readiness to answer the longings of his

1

people, if only *they* will answer the longings of his heart. Even when Israel disobeys his word, disregards his promises, scorns his love, God will not give them up: "My people are bent on turning away from me; so they are appointed to the yoke, and none shall remove it", he says in Hosea, but then immediately continues, "How can I give you up, O Ephraim! How can I hand you over, O Israel! How can I make you like Admah! How can I treat you like Zeboiim! My heart recoils within me, my compassion grows warm and tender. I will not execute my fierce anger, I will not again destroy Ephraim; for I am God and not man, the Holy One in your midst, and I will not come to destroy" (11:7-9).

"I am God and not man" — in other words, although man's pity has its limits, God's pity has no limits. Our love is conditioned by our finite nature as creatures; but his love knows no bounds. "Who is a God like thee?" asks Micah, "pardoning iniquity and passing over transgression for the remnant of his inheritance? He does not retain his anger for ever because he delights in steadfast love. He will again have compassion upon us, he will tread our iniquities under foot. Thou wilt cast all our sins into the depths of the sea. Thou wilt show faithfulness to Jacob and steadfast love to Abraham, as thou hast sworn to our fathers from the days of old" (7:18-20).

The history of salvation is, then, the history of God's wooing of his people, for, as St John reminds us, God is love. We all know that it is not possible to compel someone to love us — love cannot be bought, cannot be produced by threatening or by bribing. So, even when God does threaten his people with extinction , he recoils from carrying out the threat, for he is God and not man. Instead, he sends deliverance, in the form of judges or prophets; most fundamentally, he sends deliverance in Moses, he leads the people out of their bondage to the Egyptians, and he gives them a law on Sinai which should enable them to stay close to him in love. This law is indeed the mark of his love, as Moses says: "For what great nation is there that has a god so near to it as the

Lord our God is to us, whenever we call upon him? And what great nation is there, that has statutes and ordinances so righteous as all this law which I set before you this day?" (Deut 4:7-8). Or, as the psalmist says, "He declares his word to Jacob, his statutes and ordinances to Israel. He has not dealt thus with any other nation; they do not know his ordinances. Praise the Lord!" (147:9).

And yet the gift of the law in all its splendour, the law that was sweeter than honey in the mouth, was not enough. Not enough for God, that is to say — for he had yet more to give. If the old covenant is indeed the story of his love, it is not the whole story of his love. For there is always imperfection in man's response. God stretches out his hands, yet always the psalmist must cry, "O that today you would listen to his voice! Harden not your hearts" (94:7-8). He offers a covenant that shall last for ever, he promises rivers of living water, but he sees that his people are only too prone to hew out cisterns for themselves, "broken cisterns, that can hold no water" (Jer 2:13). As he says in Jeremiah, "The heart is deceitful above all things, and desperately corrupt; who can understand it? I the Lord search the mind and try the heart . . ." (17:9-10).

We can, then, see God in the Old Testament as trying new ways to elicit the right response from his people. When they will not respond even to his threats of exile and punishment in a far country, he permits them to suffer exile, just as earlier he had permitted the Ark of the Covenant to be taken captive by the Philistines as a punishment for the sins of the sons of Eli, Hophni and Phinehas. And in exile, he teaches them to know him through the prophecy of the Second Isaiah, he purifies them of their idolatry in Jerusalem, and finally brings them back to Israel so that there at last they may respond to his call. Yet even there, as we read in Haggai and Malachi, their response is partial at best — and at worst, they turn away from him completely. "Return to me, says the Lord of hosts, and I will return to you, says the Lord of hosts. Be not like your fathers, to whom the former prophets cried out, 'Thus says the Lord of hosts,

Return from your evil ways and from your evil deeds'"
(Zech 1:3-4). And, as we know from a later period, the gift
of the law, which God gave his people so that they could
respond fully to his choice of them and his call to them,
became surrounded by so much legalism that it became
deformed, and was no longer a means of bringing men to
him. Instead, the law became a means of separating the
holy from the profane, and so, of keeping men away from
God.

Then, an entirely new chapter is written in the story, for
at last God does hear the response he wanted: in Jesus.

We have spoken so far of God's looking for man — we
must not overlook the story of man's search for God, of the
blackness of a Jeremiah, who carried out a vocation which
he did not understand, of the bewilderment expressed in
the Book of Lamentations at the destruction of Jerusalem,
of the cries of pain and despair that ring through the Psalter.
If God found it hard to hear from man the right response to
his pleading, we must also say that *man* often found it hard
to hear from God any words that could make sense of his
misery. The words of God are so often, "Fear not": he tells
the people that he is truly a God at hand, not a God far off.
But, in the experience of his people, this is something they
cannot too often truly believe — remember the groanings of
the Israelites against Moses in the wilderness, or the lack of
understanding shown by those who worshipped the fertility
god Baal. For them, Yahweh did not measure up to ex-
pectations!

That is, perhaps, a slightly shocking way of putting it.
But on the level of the experience of the people of Israel,
it does in fact express what they felt. Remember what they
said to Jeremiah in Egypt: "As for the word which you
have spoken to us in the name of the Lord, we will not
listen to you. But we will do everything that we have vowed,
burn incense to the queen of heaven and pour out libations
to her, as we did, both we and our fathers, our kings and
our princes, in the cities of Judah and in the streets of
Jerusalem; for then we had plenty of food, and prospered,

and saw no evil. But since we left off burning incense to the queen of heaven and pouring out libations to her, we have lacked everything and have been consumed by the sword and by famine" (44:16-18). If it is true to say that, in the Old Testament, the response of the people was seen by God to be at best partial, it is also true that, for very many in Israel, God's response to their search for him was likewise at best partial. Hence, their history is a history of constant turning-away from him, to worship the sun, or idols, or Greek ideas. For them, too, an entirely new chapter must be written, so that they can hear the response they need to hear from God — otherwise, they must be dumb when the mockers say, "Where is your god *now*?" (Ps 41:10).

It is in Jesus that both God and man hear the response to their cries. For, as man, he was the first to make the perfect response to the total love of God, by his own total love; and, as God, he was the first truly clear response to the groping of man towards an ultimate answer to his pain. "In many and various ways God spoke of old to our fathers by the prophets; but in the last days he has spoken to us by a Son, whom he appointed the heir of all things" (Heb 1:1-2). The period of the partial is over, for, as Jesus died on the cross, the veil of the Temple was torn in two, from top to bottom, so that all might now have access to the sanctuary. In the old dispensation, only the high priest had access to the Holy of Holies, and he only once a year — but now that Christ, the true high priest, has come, we all have access with confidence to the throne of grace. In other words, we await no further revelation: all that God had to say has been said in his gift of Jesus. "He had still *one* other to send, his beloved Son . . ." After that, all we hear is the voice from the cloud saying, "This is my beloved Son, listen to him": and, when the cloud on the hill of transfiguration cleared away, "they lifted up their eyes, and saw no one but Jesus only" (cf. Mk 12:1ff.; Matt 17:1ff.).

It is in him that the twofold search of God for man and of man for God comes to its end. At last, there is a voice to say to the Father, "Lo, I have come to do thy will, O God"; and, at last, there is a voice to say to men, "Come to me, all who labour and are heavy laden, and I will give you rest. Take my yoke upon you, and learn from me; for I am gentle and lowly in heart, and you will find rest for your souls" (Heb 10:5ff.; Matt 11:28ff.). In Jesus, the two-way discourse between God and man finds its entire fulfilment, for, as man, he is totally open to the creator ("My food is to do the will of him who sent me", as he says in the fourth gospel), and, as God, he is totally open to his creatures ("I am the light of the world; he who follows me will not walk in darkness, but will have the light of life.").

The divinity and the humanity in him are not mingled with one another in such a way that we could think of him simply as basically God, or basically a man: in him the two natures are not confused, but are united in such a way that he is truly a man, truly one of us, and at the same time truly God, one with the Father and the Holy Spirit in the Blessed Trinity. It is fatally easy to simplify this belief, and to emphasise one pole of the mystery in such a way that the other pole is weakened: it was undeniably a dangerous tendency in ages past to forget about the humanity of Jesus, and there is undeniably a dangerous tendency today to forget about his divinity. But forget *either,* and you have a very different Jesus from the Jesus of the gospels, and the Jesus whom we acknowledge in the faith and the worship of his Church. Forget either pole of the mystery of God-made-man, and you have a Jesus who no longer stands on *both* sides of the God/man relationship, a Jesus who can speak to us as God, and who can speak to the Father as our brother. If we no longer have *this* Jesus of Nazareth, then, for us, as for those who waited for him during the unfolding of the old covenant, the new chapter in the story of God's quest for man and man's quest for God has still to be written.

If all of that sounds rather too theological, I ought perhaps to warn you that there will be a bit more theology in this book — for, as Evagrius, one of the earliest masters of the spiritual life, said, "If you pray aright, you are a theologian: if you are a theologian, you pray aright." Theology and spirituality are not ultimately to be separated: both are ways of searching for God, or, better, of letting God search for us. Our intellectual search and our search in prayer are simply two different modes of the one quest, two different ways in which we may lay ourselves open to his grace and hear his voice summoning us to conversion and action — and, above all, hear his voice wooing us in love. If we say, with the bride in the Song of Songs, "Draw me after you!" (1:4), we have to add, "And that means all of me — my intellect as well as the rest of me! I am holding nothing back!" When theology is cut adrift from spirituality, it very quickly becomes a dry, lifeless pursuit; and when spirituality is cut adrift from theology, it very quickly wanders into an insubstantial fantasy that has no roots in the demandingly tough realities of living in Christ. Both must grow together, so that we may reach what the letter to the Ephesians calls "the unity of the faith and of the knowledge of the Son of God, mature manhood, the measure of the stature of the fullness of Christ" (4:13). It is not just some part of us, a brain or a heart, that Christ has come to redeem and claim for his own, but the whole of us.

And it is in Jesus that we find this wholeness of response to God, for the first time in the history of the human race. In him, we see what man truly is, and what man truly can be; in him, we see, too, what God truly is, and what that can mean for us if we are willing to surrender ourselves to him to be remade in his likeness.

If we are willing: here is the second polarity of our prayer. For we know that we are truly redeemed in Christ, that in our baptism we have died with him and have been raised to newness of life. And yet, and yet . . . When we meet people who are genuinely holy, we do find it possible to believe all that I have just said! But when we consider ourselves, we know perfectly well that we are men and women of sin. Here is the second great tension in our spiritual lives: we are redeemed, and yet we are sinners.

It is possible to spend too much of our time lamenting individual sins. The Fathers consistently warn us that, if we find ourselves weeping over our individual sins, it is likely that what has really been hurt is not our love of God, but our own self-confidence. We thought that we had the strength to stand on our own two feet, and now we find we do not have such strength — hence our tears. If that diagnosis is correct, then we must simply pick ourselves up, and get on with living, for we are reacting far too superficially to our sins. The true problem in our lives is not individual sinful acts, but rather our sinfulness, our state of being turned away from God — the particular sins are only the manifestations of this underlying problem.

Our redemption in Christ was not the result of any good deeds of our own — it was only because God loved us so much that he sent his Son to take away our sins. Now, what does that kind of language actually *mean*, what is the value of saying "Behold, the Lamb of God, who takes away the sins of the world", if in fact we continue to sin, because our faces are set, not to go to Jerusalem and die with Jesus, but to run off and play the harlot with false gods? What can it *mean* to say that we are ransomed, that we are healed, when the evidence of our daily lives shows us that our living is built on assumptions which leave no room, or very little room, for God and his grace? "*How* can we who died to sin still live in it?" asks St Paul (Rom 6:2). I wonder if you share my reaction to that verse? I am always inclined to reply to St Paul, "Oh dear, it's terribly easy!"

The answer is not to be found in ourselves, but in Jesus. It is when Paul is in danger of thinking well of himself, as an apostle who has accomplished what by any human standards are extraordinary feats in the service of the gospel, that God sends him a thorn in the flesh to keep him in his proper place: the place of one who acknowledges, "Now I live — not I, but Christ lives in me" (Gal 2:20; cf. 2 Cor 12:1ff.). Our justification was not something God owed us for our own goodness: rather, "while we were still weak, Christ died for the *ungodly*" (Rom 5:6). We had no sort of claim upon him. Yet he came — for the language of justice and debts and things owed cannot begin to be an adequate way of speaking of God's ways with his people. He came, because he loved us: "in this the love of God was made manifest among us, that God sent his only Son into the world, so that we might live through him" (1 Jn 4:9). He sent his Son, not to take some phantasmal form of human existence untouched by our weakness, but as one like ourselves. And that means one touched by sin. He did not sin. But he was not immune from the possibility of sinning — otherwise, the temptations of which the gospels speak, in the wilderness and in the garden of Gethsemane, would be mere shams. Paul can go so far as to say that "for our sake, he made him *to be sin,* who knew no sin" (2 Cor 5:21). When God the Son came into our fallen world, he did not wear gloves to keep his hands from getting dirty. He shared our dirt, he shared our weariness, he shared — most startling of all — our radical separatedness from God, for he cried out on the cross, "My God, my God, why have you forsaken me?" A cry that was no piece of theatre, but a cry of agony. And yet, as the letter to the Hebrews tells us, he did not sin: "in every respect he has been tempted as we are, yet without sin" (4:15).

And so, we can breathe free air now. Because one of us has experienced our utter brokenness, our utter fallenness from God, and yet has *not* been corrupted as we are, has *not* yielded to the snares and flattery of sin as we do, has *not* submitted to the embrace of the sin that clings so close to us, but has turned himself always to the Father, in the very depths of his human aridness, with the trust of a child, now it is possible for *us* to be free from the grip of our sinfulness. It is not easy — Jesus did not simply turn on a switch and flood us with electric light. To imitate him, to walk in his footsteps, is to commit ourselves to carrying the cross after him. And even if we shall find that, by walking after him with the cross, we are in a mysterious way walking in a triumphal procession, yet for us there can be no escaping the pain which he endured. Those who conquer are those "who loved not their lives, even unto death"; yet always the strong paradox is felt, that it is not through their heroism as individuals that they have conquered, but "by the blood of the Lamb" (cf. Rev 12:11). In his dying and in his rising, Jesus has opened a gate for all who will to follow him. He has effected a radical change in our human situation, so that now it is truly possible for us to give God the response he seeks — and, looking at it from our human side of the fence, it is now possible for us to find in God the true response to all our needs. His face is no longer screened from view by clouds, but is revealed in the face of his Son, "for it is the God who said, 'Let light shine out of darkness', who has shone in our hearts to give the light of the knowledge of the glory of God in the face of Christ" (2 Cor 4:6).

"But," as St Paul immediately continues, "we have this treasure in earthen vessels, to show that the transcendent power belongs to God and not to us." Not to us, Lord, not to us, but to your name give the glory!

All this means that, although we are on the road, we are not yet safely home — *in via*, not yet *in patria*. And here we find the third polarity, or double movement, of our prayer: on the one hand, we look backwards, to what God has done in Christ, and, on the other hand, we look forward, to the final consummation when God shall be all in all. "Here we have no abiding city, but we seek the city which is to come" (Heb 13:14). That city, which is in process of construction as long as our human history shall last, is the new Jerusalem, the mother of us all, the bride of the Lamb, in which all our struggles will find their consummation in the day that knows no ending.

The imagery of the last chapters of the Book of Revelation, which those who do not have a taste for apocalyptic tend to pass by, is in fact saying something tremendously important to us: that while, on the one hand, it is true that everything we do has a real significance in God's sight, yet, our human history is not in itself the final word. The history of men stands under judgement, for the final word belongs to God — and that word is a word of judgement, when the evil we have done must pass through fire. So we are steadfastly to look forward — not to say, like those whom the author of 2 Peter rebukes, "Where is the promise of his coming? For ever since the fathers fell asleep, all things have continued as they were from the beginning of creation." Rather, we must fix our hopes on "the new heavens and a new earth in which righteousness dwells" (cf. 2 Pet 3). It is easy, if we give up any belief at all in future eschatology, to drown in the humdrum details of our lives. But if we really believe that the words, "Lo, I am coming like a thief! Blessed is he who is awake" (Rev 16:15), actually do contain a warning to us from Jesus, then we too, like the wise virgins of the parable, will be alert to answer the call at midnight: "Behold, the bridegroom! Come out to meet him" (cf. Matt 25:1ff.).

Of course, this expectation of a final end at the second coming of Christ must not nullify our concern with this life and its tasks — at every moment we are called to be God's fellow-workers in the ministry of reconciliation, in the building of his kingdom. But the *ultimate* significance of what we do lies not within history, but outside it, after it, when Christ delivers the kingdom to God his Father, and God is all in all. Only then does the marriage of Christ and his bride, the Church, take place, only then will the longing of God to be fully at one with his people, and the longing of men to be fully at one with their creator, find their fulfilment, when "he will wipe away every tear from their eyes, and death shall be no more, neither shall there be mourning nor crying nor pain any more, for the former things have passed away" (Rev 21:4). Our prayer as Christians in the Spirit of Jesus does not draw its strength only from the memory of the wonderful things done in the past: it draws strength, and power to overthrow all the tyranny of sin in this world, from the knowledge that the world lies under the judgement of God and that, at the last, the kingdom of this world will truly become the kingdom of our God and of his Christ, and he shall reign for ever.

This point may remind us that, when we come before God in prayer, we do not do so simply as individuals, but always as members of a family — whether it is a particular congregation, or the Church as a whole, or indeed the whole human race from Adam to the parousia. The real tragedies of sin in this world are not so much my sin, or your sin, or his sin, or her sin, but the sinfulness that transcends the capacity of any of us as individuals to heal: the sinfulness that finds its expression in war, in the economic exploitation of one group in society by another, or of one country by another, in famine which our economic and political structures could prevent if they wished, and so on. I need not give a very long list; we could all add to it with little more trouble than it takes to read this morning's newspaper. "We are members one of another", scripture tells us (Rom 12:5), and that means that we all share in the sin and the guilt. But it also means that we share in the grace and the holiness which Christ has given to his people: we all share in the potential for freedom and healing, for righteousness, which he has brought us in his dying and rising. If we know solidarity in sin, we know also solidarity in grace, for Christ died for all men, and God wishes all men to be saved and come to the knowledge of the truth. This fundamental fact has profound consequences for our prayer.

It means, in the first place, that we can never pray like the Pharisee in the parable, "I thank you that I am not like other men" (Lk 18:11). For even if the particular sins that so-and-so commits do not happen to be *my* particular sins, still I sin: and, paradoxically, as we all know, the closer we draw to God the more aware of our sins we become.

In the second place, and more importantly, it means that we can believe that our prayer does have power to do good. That is something that it is very often hard to believe; partly, no doubt, because we are so busy rejecting magical ideas about prayer that we have no time to construct an authentically Christian understanding of what it is we do when we pray. Let me express one idea, quite simply, without pretending to exhaust the reality. If we experience solidarity with our fellows in sin and in righteousness, then we must experience *change* in ourselves as other people change. To take a small example, if someone we are with receives a letter with good news, her joy makes us happy too; if my friend experiences a bereavement, I share his grief. We believe that Christ has meaning for us, not as something stuck on to the outside of our human experience, so to speak, but rather as something *internal* to our human history — he is our brother, and his triumph over death and sin makes it possible for us, in our turn, to triumph over death and sin. Now, insofar as I grow in Christ and learn to carry the cross behind him, this *must* make some kind of difference in the world — first of all, and most perceptibly, in those I meet, but then in those they meet, and so on. That difference might not, of course, be a good difference: we know how very few of us are walking advertisements for the Christian faith! But, presuming that I am growing truly in Christ, not according to some lopsided version of the gospel that suits *my* inclinations, but according to *his* call to me, then, given that we are all members one of another, we can say that things have changed in the world. A candle has been lit.

It is in prayer, in our hearing of God's word to us and our speaking to him, that any growth in Christ must be rooted. And so it is in prayer that we find our true selves, the selves which God created for us in the likeness of his Son. And it is in prayer that we have to respond to his grace, and so overcome all that keeps us away from him, all the falseness that prevents us from saying "yes" to his will. He calls to us, "Where are you?", as once he called to Adam: and we must respond, in our prayer, by coming out from the trees and permitting him to clothe our nakedness — as Jesus says in the Book of Revelation, he will give "white garments to clothe you and to keep the shame of your nakedness from being seen, and salve to anoint your eyes, that you may see" (3:18). All this must happen to us in our prayer, when we stand in the presence of God and drop the mask which we wear — the mask which for so many of us as

Christians is a good mask, a nice mask, not an ugly mask of
sin but a pleasing mask of virtue. That sort of mask is much
harder to remove than a straightforward mask of sinfulness,
and it is above all in *prayer* that the Lord can begin to get
to work on us.

There is an inescapably individual element here, for, as I
said earlier, *my* sinfulness, the things in me that are bent
and broken, will not be the same as *your* sinfulness; and the
things wrong in me today are not the things that were
wrong two years ago, nor the things that will be wrong five
years from now. Nevertheless, although it is as individuals
that we have to present ourselves to Christ the physician,
we are members one of another, and, insofar as he can
heal me, he is healing his whole Body. The Fathers have a
beautiful image for this: think of a circle with Christ at its
centre. Each of us moves towards him on a different radius
of the circle, and yet, as we each move towards him we
inescapably draw nearer to each other. For it is in him that
our human unity is grounded – not in the simple fact that
we are all human beings, but in the much more wonderful
fact that we have all one Father and that God the Son took
our humanity to himself.

We see, then, that our duty to work out our salvation
with fear and trembling is not merely an individual responsibility – it is a call to care for the whole Church of God, and
so for the whole human race. If we draw closer to one
another in drawing closer to Jesus, it is no less true that we
draw further apart from one another in drawing away from
him – for love of God and love of neighbour are insepar-
able. Remember the words of Our Lord, "As you did it to
one of the least of these my brethren, you did it to me:
as you did it not to one of the least of these, you did it not
to me" (cf. Matt 25:31ff.). He is speaking in this parable of
what we call the corporal works of mercy – but, of course,
his words apply equally to the spiritual works of mercy, to
prayer in Christ and in particular to prayer for others.

In the next chapters of this book, I would like to say
something about *how* we get down to the work of open-

ing ourselves to God in prayer, of how we permit him to put down his roots in us, and I shall concentrate on the prayer of the Psalms, which the Christian tradition has always upheld as a specially privileged way of access to God. And, bearing in mind the double movement of prayer, if it is a privileged way of access for us to God, it must also be seen as a privileged way of access for God to us — the double movement goes on inseparably. It might seem odd that Christian prayer should so emphasise the value of a collection of non-Christian hymns; why should we not sing specifically Christian hymns, which speak of Jesus and his redeeming work explicitly? To answer this, we must consider what it means to speak of Jesus as the fulfilment of God's promises in the old covenant, and I shall say something about that in the next chapter. But we might end this chapter by considering briefly the prayer of the Psalms in relation to the four double movements in the spiritual life which I have sketched.

First, the movement of God towards man and the movement of man towards God. It is obvious that the Psalms bear witness to this double movement, for some of them address God, while others give the words of God to men. Others again constitute a sort of dialogue between two speakers. To say more about this involves speaking about the work of Christ; here, let me simply say that, at least on the most obvious level, that of literary form, the prayers in the Psalter show us the double movement of which I have spoken.

The same is true of the next double movement — the polarity between being redeemed and being sinners. There are many passages of the Psalms which speak of being rescued and brought into freedom, for example Psalm 125, which celebrates the return of the exiles from Babylon to Jerusalem, or Psalm 106, the long song which celebrates the deliverance which God has brought in so many various ways to his faithful. But equally, there are many passages which speak of the sin and the backsliding of Israel, for example Psalm 80, in which the Lord laments the ingratitude of his people ("My people did not listen to my voice; Israel would have none of me."), or Psalm 50, the classic prayer of repentance. (See chapter 5 below.) Thanksgiving and repentance are each integral to the prayers of the Psalter.

Third, we can look backwards in the Psalms, as in Psalm 80 to the deliverance from Egypt, or in Psalm 125 to the return from Babylon; and we can also look forward, as in Psalm 13: "O that deliverance for Israel would come out of Zion! When the Lord restores the fortunes of his people, Jacob shall rejoice, Israel shall be glad"; or, as in Psalm 42, with its refrain: "Hope in God; for I shall again praise him, my help and my God."

Fourth, when we think of the duality of individual and community, we may remember that very frequently in the Psalms the "I" is not exclusively to be understood as an individual, such as the Davidic king, but should also be seen to include the people. And conversely, when the poet speaks in the plural, he does not exclude himself – the sorrows or joys of Israel are his sorrows or joys too.

The Psalter, therefore, in its literary forms and its subject matter, constantly reminds us of these four movements of our prayer. And this reminder comes all the more strongly when the Psalms are our daily prayer, in the Mass or the office or our private prayers. But does that make the Psalms *Christian* prayers? It is not enough to reply that, as a matter of historical fact, the Psalms have always been prayed by Christians, or that we take them as inspired scripture: there is a whole Christological question here. The teaching of the Fathers of the Church has, in my judgement, much to teach *us* in the twentieth century. I shall try in the remainder of this book to bring out something of the richness of their understanding for us, as we pray the Psalms of David which they prayed in their day.

2 Christ, the end of the law

In the first chapter of St John's Gospel, when Philip finds his friend Nathanael, he says to him, "We have found him of whom Moses in the law and also the prophets wrote, Jesus of Nazareth, the son of Joseph." And in the last chapter of St Luke's Gospel, when Jesus meets the two disciples who are walking to Emmaus, he says to them, "O foolish men, and slow of heart to believe all that the prophets have spoken! Was it not necessary that the Christ should suffer these things and enter into his glory?" And St Luke continues, "And beginning with Moses and all the prophets, he interpreted to them in all the scriptures the things concerning himself."

So we can see the story of Jesus in the gospels as framed by the statement that he is the one about whom Moses and the prophets spoke in the old covenant. As St Paul says, "all the promises of God find their Yes in him. That is why we utter the Amen through him, to the glory of God" (2 Cor 1:20). What this means for us, as Christian believers who read the Old Testament, is that the key which will unlock its meaning is not contained somewhere within the text itself, but is outside it: for, as St Paul says later on in 2 Corinthians, "when a man turns to *the Lord* the veil is removed" (3:16). It is only through Jesus that we can understand what the true meaning of the Old Testament is for us. "You search the scriptures", says Jesus in St John's Gospel, "because you think that in them you have eternal life; and it is they that bear witness to *me* . . . if you believed Moses, you would believe me, for he wrote of *me*" (5:39, 46).

If we are to make our own the prayers of the Psalter, we can do so as Christians only in the light of this conviction: that in Jesus Christ, the Son of God and Son of Mary, the words of God in the old covenant have been fulfilled. Fine, we might say to that; but what, precisely, does this idea of "fulfilment" mean? I would like to begin to answer that question by looking briefly at the antiphons which we sing at the Magnificat during vespers on the last days before Christmas (17-23 December). These seven antiphons contain implicitly a very rich understanding of Jesus as the fulfiller of the scriptures.

On 17 December, we sing *O Sapientia:* "O wisdom that came forth from the mouth of the Most High, reaching from one end to the other, strongly and sweetly disposing all things: come to teach us the way of prudence!"

On 18 December, we sing *O Adonai:* "O Adonai and captain of the house of Israel, who appeared to Moses in the fire of the flaming bush, and gave him the law on Sinai: come to redeem us with outstretched arm!"

On 19 December, we sing *O radix Iesse:* "O root of Jesse, who stand as an ensign of the peoples, at whom kings shall shut their mouths, whom the peoples acclaim: come to free us, delay now no longer!"

On 20 December, we sing *O clavis David:* "O key of David, and sceptre of the house of Israel; you open, and no one closes; you close, and no one opens: come and lead out from the prison-house him who is bound and sits in darkness and the shadow of death!"

On 21 December, we sing *O Oriens:* "O Dayspring, splendour of eternal light and sun of justice: come, and give light to those who sit in darkness and the shadow of death!"

On 22 December, we sing *O Rex gentium:* "O king of the peoples, whom they desire; corner-stone, who make the two one: come and save the man whom you fashioned out of clay!"

Finally, on 23 December, we sing *O Emmanuel:* "O Emmanuel, our king and lawgiver, desire of the peoples, and their saviour: come to save us, Lord our God!"

The images, the echoes of scripture, tumble over one another in these antiphons — it is as if we cannot find

enough titles to give to Christ while we cry out to him
breathlessly: *Veni,* "Come!" The cry of the Spirit and the
Bride, the cry "Come, Lord Jesus!" which closes the Book
of Revelation, is echoed in these antiphons as the Church
sings the song of Our Lady, which St Luke tells us she
sang while she waited for the birth of her son — and, in a
mysterious way, we move out of our own time and find
that we are singing with the men and women of the old
covenant who waited for a saviour; we are singing with
Mary, as she waited for the birth of the saviour whom she
bore in her womb; and we are singing with all the Church
through the ages, which cries, "Maranatha! Our Lord,
come!", as she waits for the second coming in glory of the
Saviour who will bring an end to sin and death, and take us
to himself. "When I go and prepare a place for you, I will
come again and will take you to myself, that where I am
you may be also" (Jn 14:3).

That can all sound very heady — we might turn our
thoughts so resolutely to the triumphant second coming in
glory that we forget the first coming in lowliness, the first
coming when "he came to his own, and his own received
him not" (Jn 1:11). But the promise of Jesus in the farewell discourses of John, "Where I am you shall be also", is
in fact always a call to martyrdom, to suffering as Jesus
suffered: "He who loves his life loses it, and he who hates
his life in this world will keep it for eternal life. If anyone
serves me, he must follow me; and where I am, there shall
my servant be also; if any one serves me, the Father will
honour him" (Jn 12:25-26). The waiting of Israel for its
Messiah was no easy time for them, but was a long succession
of doubts and disasters and pain; the waiting of the Church
for the second coming of the Saviour is no easy time for
us, but a time when weeds and wheat are growing up
together, and we must be constantly on the watch.

The great beauty of the season of Advent is that it
reminds us of this double waiting: Israel's waiting for a
deliverance which they dimly understood, and our waiting
for a deliverance which we dimly understand. "Here we

walk by faith, not by sight" (2 Cor 5:7): we are not yet
fully in possession of "what no eye has seen, nor ear heard,
nor the heart of man conceived" (1 Cor 2:9). In a real sense
we can say that, in our Christian experience of life in the
Holy Spirit, we have the foretaste of the glory that one day
will be revealed; but it remains always true that we are in a
value of tears — as St Paul says, "Here indeed we *groan*, and
long to put on our heavenly dwelling" (2 Cor 5:2). The life
of the Christian is always the life of an exile in this world —
it is a world that we must love, a world that is the good
creation of a loving Father, a world that is held in being
by the word of God, and yet it is a world of which the
letter of James can say, "Do you not know that friendship
with the world is enmity with God? Therefore whoever
wishes to be a friend of the world makes himself an enemy
of God" (4:4). And the first letter of Peter addresses us as
"aliens and exiles" (2:11).

So our condition is really very similar to that of the first
Israel, the chosen people who waited for a redemption that
would bring them to be truly what they were called to be —
the children of God. If I may use the language I used in the
last chapter, they longed to stretch out their hands to their
Father; and *he* longed to stretch out his hands and hold
them. Finally, in Jesus heaven and earth became one. And
yet, as the letter to the Hebrews reminds us, although God
has indeed put everything in subjection to his Son, "we do
not yet *see* everything in subjection to him" (2:8). In every
generation, we have to struggle so that he may truly be lord
— not that he may simply have the title "Lord, Lord", but
that he may genuinely be the ruler of the hearts of men.
And our hope must be turned to him, to the fullness of his
salvation — a salvation which we now experience in our
baptism, in the sacraments of the Church, in our life of
prayer, in what Hebrews call our "tasting of the powers
of the age to come" (6:5), but a salvation that still awaits
its final accomplishment. Always, we live with imperfection,
with brokenness, with sin: always, in this life, we must turn
our eyes to him and to his future deliverance. So we are

not very different from the men of Israel who waited for him. They did not know his name as yet: we do know his name, and *he* has called us by name as he called Mary Magdalene by name in the garden on Easter morning. If, then, we know him by name, and know that his love for us has no limits, then we must be all the more earnest in our prayer, "O Dayspring, splendour of eternal light and sun of justice: *come,* and give light to those who sit in darkness and the shadow of death!"

If it is true to say that our position as Christians who await the coming in glory of the risen Lord is not *altogether* different from the position of the Jews who waited for his first coming, then clearly we can make their language our own. We must certainly not forget that there *is* a massive difference! "Blessed are your eyes, for they see, and your ears, for they hear" (Matt 13:16). This fuller knowledge carries its own responsibilities: "The men of Nineveh will arise at the judgement with this generation and condemn it," says Jesus, "for they repented at the preaching of Jonah, and behold, something greater than Jonah is here. The queen of the south will arise at the judgement with this generation and condemn it; for she came from the ends of the earth to hear the wisdom of Solomon, and behold, something greater than Solomon is here" (Matt 12:41-2). Just as the first Israel was God's priestly people, with the duty to make known his name among the peoples of the world, so the second Israel, the Church, must make his name known: "Woe to me, if I do not preach the gospel!" (1 Cor 9:16).

Now that Jesus has come, we can put a name to the loving kindness of God — we can understand that the prophecies of the old covenant must be read (indeed, can only be read) in the light of *his* coming. "He explained to them in all the scriptures *ta peri heautou,* the things concerning *himself*", says St Luke (24:27). For the scriptures of the old covenant bear witness to the steadfast love of God, who has bound himself in a bond of unshakable fidelity to the people whom he chose. And the ultimate proof of that love is Jesus — no external manifestation of that love, but indeed the very stuff of that love, for he and the Father are one: "Have I been with you so long, and yet you do not know me, Philip? He who has seen me has seen the Father" (Jn 14:9). "Fear not," he says to John in the vision which opens the Book of Revelation, "I am the first and the last, and the living one" (1:17-18); he is the Alpha and the Omega, who was before all things, and in whom all things find the principle of their very existence. "He is the image of the invisible God, the first-born of all creation; for in him all things were created, in heaven and on earth, visible and invisible . . . all things were created through him and for him. He is before all things, and in him all things hold together" (Col 1:15-17). "All things were made through him, and without him was not anything made that was made. In him was life" (Jn 1:3-4).

"All things were made *for* him", says the letter to the Colossians. And so we may understand the whole unfolding of the relationship of love between God and his people in the old covenant as a preparation for the full flowering of that revelation in the incarnation of God the Son.

All things were made for him; and "all things were made *through* him". That is why the Advent antiphon can address Jesus and say, "Come and save the man whom you fashioned out of clay!" Very early on, the Church understood the words of Gen 1:26, "Let us make man in our image, after our likeness", as addressed by the Father to the Son — so that, when God looked on the face of Adam, he recognised there the form of his own image and likeness, of his own Son who is eternally begotten in the Trinity.

All things were made for him, and all things were made through him — it is also true that "*in* him all things hold together". That is why the Advent antiphon can address Jesus and say, "You reach from one end to the other, strongly and sweetly disposing all things" (cf. Wis 8:1). And this act of sustaining all things in existence is not some kind of impersonal force at work in the universe, but something that involves the Son personally: that is why the anti-

phon can say to him, "O Adonai, and captain of the house
of Israel, who appeared to Moses in the fire of the flaming
bush, and gave him the law on Sinai: come to redeem us
with outstretched arm!" It is the Son who is the word
of God's revelation to men, the revelation in the physical
world ("The heavens are telling the glory of God", as
Psalm 18 says), but above all in the history of Israel's en-
counter with God.

For the Hebrew, God is, above all, the God of the "outstretched arm", who reveals himself most clearly and charac-
teristically in what he *does.* He is a God at hand, and not a
God far off: a God who rides on the heavens to come to the
defence of his beloved people. The idols of the Gentiles,
which have feet but cannot move, are powerless to save
those who trust in them — but the Lord of Israel, who is a
God who *acts,* will rescue all who call on his name. This
revelation of who God is is, of course, incomplete in the
period of the old covenant; and still today, we see as in a
mirror, dimly, and not yet face to face. But we are no longer
stumbling in darkness, putting our trust in a God who
might seem to have withdrawn from us — now, we know
the name by which he wishes to be addressed; now, he has
sent into our hearts the Spirit of his Son, so that we too
may address him as "Abba". In Jesus, we come to know the
underlying unity of all things, we come to understand how
it is possible for all things in the cosmos to speak to us of
their maker, and of him who sustains them. In Jesus, then,
we hear the "Yes" to all the promises of God. In him, the
shadows have cleared, and the sun of righteousness has risen.

If we read the Old Testament in the light of this understanding, we find that it is indeed our book. Nevertheless,
we must continually bear in mind that this is not a book
written after the coming of Jesus, but before it; and it
is quite clear that one of the effects of the coming of Jesus
was to supersede part of what went before. "When the
perfect comes, the imperfect will pass away", says Paul
(1 Cor 13:10) — as we sing in the liturgy for Corpus Christi
Day: *Vetustatem novitas, umbram fugat veritas.* (The new-

ness puts the oldness to flight, the truth chases away the
shadow.) When *we* read the law of Moses, we do not read
it as a detailed code of commandments which we ourselves
are to obey; for example, when *we* read Leviticus, we do
not then get up and go off to sacrifice a goat. The coming
of Christ has made some things in the old covenant no
longer needed as mediators of the presence of God: when
he who is the Light of the world is present, we do not need
to make do with lesser illumination.

This point is important when we think of the prayer of
the Psalms, because the assumption that we can simply take
over all the Psalms and use them as Christian prayers, without further ado, is an assumption that needs questioning.
There are passages in the Psalter that no Christian ought to
feel comfortable with, as, for example, in Psalm 136: after
the lament over his exile far from the holy city, with the
words "Let my tongue cleave to my mouth, if I do not
remember you, if I do not set Jerusalem above my highest
joy!", the psalmist fiercely curses the Edomites and the
Babylonian captors, ending with the words, "Happy shall
he be who takes your little ones and dashes them against
the rock!" It seems to me that any Christian who can *pray*
such terrible words is a Christian who, to borrow St Paul's
phrase, "does not yet know as he ought to know" (cf. 1 Cor
8:2). It is entirely right that in the new Breviary we do not
pray these verses. It is, of course, true that some sort of
sense can be twisted out of them, if we take the traditional
line of interpreting the "little ones" as evil thoughts which
are to be dashed to pieces on the rock which is Christ; but
the very contortedness of such an interpretation seems to
me to be a good indication that it has nothing to be said in
its favour.

It remains true that such passages of cursing one's
enemies are part of the canon of scripture; and we may
remember the words of 2 Timothy, "All scripture is inspired
by God and profitable for teaching, for reproof, for correc-
tion, and for training in godliness, that the man of God may
be complete, equipped for every good work" (3:16-17).

But we are not told here that every passage of scripture contains a sentiment or a prayer that we are to make our own: if I were asked what value texts like Psalm 57, with its elaborate and disgusting curses, have for the spiritual life of the Christian, I should reply that their value is precisely that they teach us what we should *not* do, what we should *not* be feeling! And that, after all, is what Jesus teaches us in the antitheses of the Sermon on the Mount: for example, "You have heard that it was said, 'You shall love your neighbour and hate your enemy'. But *I* say to you, love your enemies and pray for those who persecute you, so that you may be sons of your Father who is in heaven; for he makes his sun rise on the evil and on the good, and sends rain on the just and on the unjust" (Matt 5:43-45). The divine authority of Jesus, "You have heard . . . but *I* say to you", sets aside the literal teaching of the law. He has this authority because, when he speaks, it is the voice of God that we hear; we remember the Advent antiphon, "O Adonai and captain of the house of Israel, who appeared to Moses in the fire of the flaming bush, and gave him the law on Sinai . . ."

He did not come to abolish the law, but to bring it to perfection by instilling in our hearts the new commandment to love one another "as I have loved you" (Jn 13:34). That is a love which knows no calculation of precisely how much I owe this other person, or he owes me — it is a love which lays down one's life for one's friends. After the Resurrection, Jesus did not ask Peter, "Simon, son of John, are you sorry that you broke the law by betraying me?" He asked him quite simply, "Simon, son of John, do you love me?" (cf. Jn 21:15ff.). *This* is the new law, the new principle of living which supersedes the older law, not by abolishing it and setting up a different code of regulations in its place, but by giving expression to what was the underlying principle of the Torah — love. God gave Israel the law because he loved his people: in the traditional Jewish interpretation of the Song of Songs, the love celebrated in the poetry is the love which led God to give Israel the Torah. The law was

given so that man and God could be at one. But, since that
gift was insufficient, a higher law was needed — the law
which Jesus proclaimed when he laid down his life for his
sheep, "leaving you an example, that you should follow in
his steps" (1 Pet 2:21). The new covenant does not abolish
what was good in the old: it abolishes only what was imperfect, what men had turned to their own ends. It is no longer
the law of Moses that is the evidence of God's love for his
creatures; in the Christian interpretation of the Song of
Songs, the love celebrated in the poetry is the love of Christ
and his bride the Church, who are now fully at one: "My
beloved is mine and I am his" (2:16).

This fact, that not every verse of the Old Testament is of
equal force in the light of the Incarnation and the giving
of a new covenant in the blood of Jesus, means that we
need not try to squeeze an edifying meaning or a profound
Christological insight out of every verse in the Psalms. It
can be rather tiresome to read through the lengthy patristic
commentaries on the Psalter, precisely because the Fathers
had such a hard time trying to make it *all* read as a Christian
text. I should myself prefer to admit that there are senti-
ments expressed in the Psalter, as elsewhere in the Old
Testament, which we must not make our own, just as there
are prayers that we dare not pray, if we are to be true to
the fullness of God's revelation in his incarnate Son. But
such texts in the Psalter are extremely rare — with the over-
whelming majority of the Psalms, there is no difficulty for
us in praying these words of the old covenant, and the added
richness of praying as disciples of Jesus in the fellowship
of his Church does not diminish their own intrinsic spiritual
value as prayers. Rather, we can move on two levels (at
least!) as we pray, conscious that we are part of a long
tradition of praying these Psalms, and making the fullest
use of the resources of that tradition.

For us, that may well mean making use of modern commentaries on the Psalms, for we must never neglect the
literal meaning. It is often hard to work out what the
original situation envisaged by the psalmist was; and indeed,

since many of the older Psalms were used in the Davidic
Temple, in the period of exile, and in the restored Temple,
the question is not really, "What original situation is
envisaged?", but rather, "Which situation in Hebrew worship should I have in mind to help me understand this
hymn?" In any case, we must not isolate the Psalms from
their original setting, for to do that is to risk cutting ourselves
loose from our own origins. We are the children of Abraham,
and when we pray the Psalms we stand in continuity with
all of his other children who composed these hymns and
sang them in the house of the God of Abraham, Isaac and
Jacob at Jerusalem. The Fathers, in their day, were aware
that we must not neglect the literal meaning of the words
we sing.

Nevertheless, for the Christian at prayer, the literal
meaning is not the primary meaning; and this is true in
general of the Old Testament scriptures when we pray.
The *sensus plenior,* the sense in which the scriptures have
come to their fulfilment in Jesus Christ, is the very reason
we pray with these texts at all: it is because he has lit them
up from within; because, in them, we hear his voice; because, in St Paul's words, "these things were written down
for *our* instruction" (1 Cor 10:11). And, as we pray the
Psalms, it is valuable to realise that we stand in continuity
with Christians who have prayed them for many centuries;
we acknowledge a fundamental fact of our Christian living:
that we do not belong to the first generation of believers,
but take our places in the long line of those who have gone
before us, and, in turn, hand on to those who follow us our
testimony about what the Lord has done. In all that we do
as disciples of Jesus of Nazareth — in our belief, in our worship, in our ethics — we come up against that simple fact
of givenness. It was there before you and me, and it will be
there when you and I are forgotten.

This duty of passing on the faith, of giving account of
the hope that is in us, is something that we all know. St Paul
was a man supremely aware of his ministry to teach and to
nurture those who were babes in Christ, but he did not see

it as a one-way process in which he had to do all the giving,
and his disciples had to do all the receiving: he writes to
the Romans, "I long to see you, that I may impart to you
some spiritual gift to strengthen you, that is, that we may
be mutually encouraged by each other's faith, both yours
and mine" (1:11-12). Every teacher knows that he or she
learns much from those who are taught, and it is one sign
of St Paul's greatness as a teacher that he acknowledged
that he learned from his hearers. Nevertheless, even if it
is true that we *all* have this duty to teach, we still tend to
look for teaching from someone who, above all, impresses
us as one who does know the Lord. Mary Magdalene told
the disciples, "I have seen the Lord" (Jn 20:18), and so she
became what tradition calls *apostola apostolorum*, "the
apostle of the apostles". In every generation, we turn
instinctively to those men and women who can say to us,
"I have seen the Lord" – and even if they shut themselves
away from the crowds, they will be found, just as Jesus
was found. Do you remember those very comforting words
in St Mark's Gospel, "He entered a house, and would not
have any one know it; yet *he* could not be hid" (7:24)?
All through his ministry, he commanded those whom he
healed to be silent about him, but of course they never
obeyed! And in our own day, we can point to St Thérèse
of Lisieux, who managed to remain hidden during her life-
time in a Carmelite convent, but who brought, after her
death, the message of a highly exacting (yet very accessible)
Christian spirituality to millions of people. We all draw
strength from those who can say to us, "I have seen the
Lord."

This is not only a question of direct personal contact
with our own contemporaries. We take our place in a long
line of believers which stretches back to the very first of the
eyewitnesses who handed on by word of mouth the story of
what Jesus had done and taught, long before there were any
written gospels or epistles. And, when we look for guidance
in our quest for God, the Fathers of the Church have a
prominent claim on us. In many respects, we could, perhaps,

fancy that we know more about the scriptures than they
did — think of all the archaeological discoveries that have
cast so much light on the Old Testament, for example. But
that would be a superficial judgement — for, in the Fathers,
there is nothing of that terrifying gulf between theology and
spirituality which has been the curse of later generations in
the Church. Today, it is possible to know a great deal about
the Bible, but to know very little of the word of God. This
has, of course, always been possible — it is perhaps one of
those perennial problems of Christian living, and one that
hits intellectuals particularly hard — but, in the period of
the Fathers, the rot had not spread as far as it has among
us, with very grave consequences both for theology and for
spirituality in the life of the Christian community. Virtually
all of the great patristic writers were bishops who wrote
their theology in the form of sermons to their people —
most of the patristic commentaries on books of the Bible
are homilies that gradually worked their way through the
text. The Fathers were steeped in scripture in a way that
scarcely any of us are — they really did know the Bible
thoroughly, and the world in which they lived was still
very much the world of the biblical writers.

That said, we must concede that it is not possible for
us somehow to skip back across the hedge of the centuries
that separate us from the Fathers — the spectacles with
which we read the Bible cannot be their spectacles. For
example, there is a view of women and of human sexuality
expressed in much patristic writing that we could never
possibly make our own today. And, time and again as one
reads the Fathers, one is reminded that we do inhabit a
different world. Nevertheless, the similarities are much
more prominent than the differences. They, too, tried to
walk in the footsteps of Jesus; they, too, reflected on the
word of God in the scriptures; they too were nourished by
the liturgical prayer of the Church; they too fought sin and
slackness.

They reflected on St Paul's teaching, "Pray constantly"
(1 Thess 5:17), and on the example of Jesus who spent

whole nights in prayer; and much of their spiritual teaching
is designed to help us put this into practice. The idea of the
mnêmê Theou, the "remembrance of God" is central to the
theology of prayer of the great tradition of the eastern
Fathers; it finds expression, for example, in the monastic
ideal which imitated the sleepless adoration of the angels
by passing whole nights in uninterrupted prayer. How can
we truly fulfil the command to pray without ceasing, to
keep the Lord ever before our eyes, as Psalm 15 says? That
is the central question which this immensely rich tradition
asks, and the answers that the Fathers found are answers *we*
cannot ignore in our search for God. It is, indeed, a glory
of the Christian tradition that it has always been redis-
covering this emphasis on constant prayer; and in western
Christianity in our times, the spread of the practice of the
"Jesus Prayer", due largely to the translations of the Russian
Way of a Pilgrim, has given many believers in our culture
access to traditions of prayer which were certainly not dead
in the west, but equally certainly were not thriving.

When the Fathers speak of the Psalms, they do so in the
light of their quest for unbroken awareness of the presence
of God — all the theological reflections generated in their
study of the Psalms have an ultimately practical point to
them. "My eyes are ever toward the Lord, for he will
pluck my feet out of the net", says the psalmist (24:15).
If he plucks my feet out of the net, he will do so only
through his Son — again we are reminded that Christian
prayer is prayer in the Spirit of Jesus Christ, that "remembrance of God" is a remembrance of the Father of Jesus.
The Fathers' awareness of salvation, their whole trust in
the help of God in the battle against slackness and sin, came
from their confidence that, in his Son, God had stretched
out his hand to sinners and so fulfilled all his promises to
Abraham and the prophets. And, in the Christian's life,
prayer is not some optional activity — all right for the Marys
but not necessary for the Marthas; no, prayer is the very
stuff and fabric of the life of the disciple of Jesus.

Various symbolic meanings became attached to the

different hours of prayer during the day, as we see in the writings of St Basil the Great, the father of eastern monasticism, or in the prayers of the new Roman Breviary (especially at Prayer During the Day on weekdays). We should pray at the third hour to remember the descent of the Holy Spirit on the apostles, and so on. The basic principle here is that of the sanctification of time: Christ has filled all things with light and life in his rising from the tomb, and always and everywhere we must be alert, rejoicing in his presence with those he redeemed. If we do set aside particular times of the day to be hours of prayer, we must also continually offer sacrifice on the altar of our heart: for God is everywhere, and in every place he must be adored; at all hours, his salvific power is at work in his world, and, at all hours, we must turn to him and open ourselves to his word.

He has filled all things with his presence. And so, when we speak of fulfilment, we must not confine our attention to the fulfilment in Jesus of the old covenant with Israel. In him, through whom and for whom all things were made, every longing of the hearts of men finds its fulfilment, every question receives its answer. In him, the deaf are given hearing, the blind receive their sight, the poor have good news preached to them — and this does not depend on the cultural or religious predispositions that they have. If Jesus is the fulfilment of the Old Testament, he is also the fulfilment of the religious aspirations of all men, for *he* cannot be kept bound. He has broken the bars of death once and for all time in his resurrection, and he has brought with him a multitude of captives, those who were held bound in their ignorance, in their fragmentary glimpses of truth and freedom and love. Wherever there is good in the world, its presence must be attributed to him; wherever there is sin, his gospel must be proclaimed, so that men may repent and find healing for their wounds. Wherever men are at ease and comfortable, they must be called to shoulder the yoke of Christ; wherever they are downtrodden, they must be relieved by hearing his call, "Come to me."

Of necessity, we can speak only about one thing at a time. It may be different in heaven, but here we cannot be thinking about everything at once! When, however, we address our thoughts to the prayer of the Psalms, and try to see how that prayer is shot through with the glory of the presence of Jesus, let us not totally forget those who do not yet know his name. Let us bear them too in our prayer, and say with the psalmist, "May God be gracious to us and bless us and make his face to shine upon us; that your way may be known upon earth, your saving power to *all* nations. Let the peoples praise you, O God; let all the peoples praise you!" (66:1-4).

3 The king will desire . . .

There is a whole tradition of spirituality that is designed to keep us in our places, to prevent us from thinking of ourselves more highly than we ought to think. "If any man thinks that he stands," says St Paul, "let him take care lest he fall!" (1 Cor 10:12). And the writings of the fathers of the monastic life are full of warnings that aspiring monks must be tested to see whether or not they are able to bear humiliations; the whole life of a monk or nun must be a turning away from pride and a delight in obscurity and hiddenness, for the spirit of vainglory is among the most dangerous temptations. All this, of course, is not designed to break the aspiring monk or nun, but rather to pierce the crust of selfishness, the crust that prevents God from really getting to work and burning out of our hearts all the rubbish in them that hinders us from fulfilling the promises we made at baptism, to reject evil and serve him. We are in a desperate state, fallen and weak and the prey of many temptations, and a desperate state requires severe remedies — hence the severity of the ascetic life, hence the severity of the early Rules of the monastic houses. But all of this, let it be said again, has ultimately a positive intention. In baptism, Jesus the second Adam has claimed us for himself, and it is the whole task of the Christian to conform his life to the reality of the eternal life which is given him when he passes through the waters of the font. Baptism is a dying with Christ, in order to be raised with him to the fullness of life — and the baptised must die every day, so that, more and more, Christ may take us to himself and make us truly his own.

As things are (and as we ourselves recognise when we are

honest), we are sinners. "I know that nothing good dwells within me," says St Paul, "that is, within my flesh. I can will what is right, but I cannot do it. For I do not do the good I want, but the evil I do not want is what I do" (Rom 7:18-19). And there he speaks for all of us — we all know, and know more and more unavoidably as we begin to move towards God, that we are sinful, that there is something twisted in us that prevents us from making the response we should to the love of God. The psalmist asks us, "How long will you love vain words, and seek after lies?" (4:2). And we must reply, "I know that nothing good dwells within me." Here, then, we have the acute tension, which is so profoundly a part of our Christian experience, between the fact that we have been redeemed by the death and resurrection of Jesus, and the fact that we remain in bondage to sin. We have, accordingly, no cause to pat ourselves on the back and say what splendid people we are: rather, we must number ourselves with those whom the second letter to Timothy calls "lovers of pleasure rather than lovers of God, people who hold the form of religion but deny the power of it" (3:4-5). With the psalmist, we must wonder, "What is man, that you take notice of him?" (143:3).

And yet, all is not black. Whenever I am tempted to give up hope, to think that there is simply no possibility of my ever saying "yes" to God and serving him, he reminds me sharply that that is the wrong kind of question to ask. I did not ask to be born into the world: the responsibility for that belongs to my parents, whose love gave birth to me. Similarly, I did not ask to be redeemed: the responsibility for that belongs to God, whose love gave me a second birth in his Son. I could not possibly have done anything to deserve being born, and I could not possibly have done anything to deserve being reborn: in both cases, it is a free gift to me of the love of someone else. "When the goodness and loving kindness of God our Saviour appeared, he saved us, not because of deeds done by *us* in righteousness, but in virtue of his own mercy, by the washing of regeneration and renewal in the Holy Spirit, which he poured out upon us richly through Jesus Christ our Saviour, so that we might be justified by his grace and become heirs in hope of eternal life" (Tit 3:4-7). The really important question in our life as disciples of Jesus is not, "What have *I* done to deserve this?", or even, "How shall *I* repay the Lord for all his goodness to me?", but rather, "How may I cooperate with the grace of God which he gives me, so that *he* may work in me whatever is pleasing to him?" Always, the initiative is from God.

But it remains true that this is an initiative of *love,* not some kind of siege of our wills, nor a showering of gifts from the king upon the beggar-maid in such a way that the true independence of the beggar-maid is obliterated. No, always God is the wooer of our souls, who looks to us for our response: "Arise, my love, my fair one, and come away; for lo, the winter is past, the rain is over and gone . . ." (Song 2:10-11). It is up to us whether or not we will reply to him: "Set me as a seal upon your heart, as a seal upon your arm; for love is as strong as death . . ." (Song 8:7). It is up to *us:* he will not force us to accept his love. But if we do open our hearts to him, he will come and make his home in them; if we do open our mouths he will fill them; and so we shall pass from death to life. Always, the initiative is God's: but he cannot make our response for us. We must do that ourselves.

If we do reply to his voice summoning us to throw off everything that hinders us and to run in the track of his footprints, then we shall find that we do truly become what he means us to be. We shall indeed begin to live out the pledges of our baptism. This, as we all know, involves a fearsomely long process of purification – often, all we can do is to hang on and trust that he *is* at work in us, even though we seem to ourselves to be as sinful as ever; even, when we find that we are committing new sins that we never committed before we began to say "yes" to God. There is nothing particularly surprising in that. It is the universal experience of the Christian tradition that we are tempted above all when we begin to let God get to work in our hearts — before that, we are not worth the devil's efforts; why should he bother to tempt *us?* And that insight remains true, whatever we may think of the demonology in which the Fathers expressed it: the more we progress towards the kingdom of heaven, the more we shall be tempted. As Paul reminded his congregations, "we must enter the kingdom of God through many tribulations" (Acts 14:22) — there are no short-cuts. Even when we seem to see men and women get there by an easy route, that is sure to be deceptive: a cross that *I* could carry without trouble may be an almost intolerable burden for someone else.

It is against the background of these reflections that I would like to meditate on Psalm 44, the wedding-song of a king and princess. The Christological interpretation of this psalm is very ancient — it can be found in the first chapter of the letter to the Hebrews; and the Christian writers of the second century were unanimous in interpreting it as an allegory of the marriage of Christ and his bride, the Church. Later writers see it as speaking of the individual Christian, or of Our Lady. Let me begin by saying something about the second part of this psalm, the verses addressed to the princess, and then I shall say something about the first part, the verses addressed to the king.

I began this chapter by observing that much of our tradition of spirituality warns us against thinking that we are beautiful people spiritually. But here we have the words, "Listen, O daughter, give ear to my words: forget your own people and your father's house. So will the king desire your beauty." The king will desire your beauty — can that be speaking of us? Our experience of sinfulness, of continual falling-short of the precepts of God, would surely forbid us to apply those words to ourselves. It must be of the Church that the poet speaks, not of you and me.

Here, of course, is the big danger for Catholics: we speak as if "the Church" was something out there, something essentially different from you and me. As if by some instinct, we tend to say, "The Church teaches us

that . . .", instead of, "We believe that . . ." But this will
not do. *We* are the Church, and all that concerns the Church
in the scriptures is of concern to us. It is true, and very
important, that no particular grouping is the whole Church;
we form only a small number of those who live in Christ,
those here on earth in the communion of the Church, and
those who have gone before us marked with the sign of
faith and stand in the presence of God. And so not everything that is addressed to the Church in the New Testament,
or implicitly in the Old Testament, is directly relevant to
you and me. But there is a big danger for us if we always
speak of "the Church" in a way that suggests we are not
speaking about ourselves — the kind of thing that you some-
times hear in sermons, when the preacher laments the danger
to the Church of the false teaching of progressives, or the
blindness of conservatives, or attacks "the Church" as
hopelessly corrupt. It is clear that such a preacher or writer
regards himself as not being a part of what he calls "the
Church", for, if he did truly so regard himself, he would be
personally involved in the sufferings of the Body of Christ.
As Christians, the dangers which arise from our human
nature are very real, dangers of a teaching which concen-
trates too narrowly on one aspect of the truth, dangers of
sinfulness in high places, dangers of laxity and indifference
— but these are dangers which threaten each of us, you and
me, dangers against which you and I must fight first of all
in ourselves. And they are dangers which will be defeated
only by the power of Christ in us; not by waving banners,
nor by forming pressure-groups, but by laying ourselves
open to the transforming power of Christ. And, if the risks
and dangers are surmounted in him, then it can be true of
you and me (not just of "the Church") that the king will
desire our beauty.

It is a beauty that is his own gift to us, a beauty given
to us in our creation in his own image, and restored to us
in the redemption of mankind in his Son. So it is never
something for which we ourselves could take the credit:
yet it is something that does really belong to us. He looks

on us, and he desires us. And so he urges us, you and me
and the whole of his Church: "Forget your own people and
your father's house." Like Abraham, who was urged, "Go
from your country and your kindred and your father's
house to the land that I will show you" (Gen 12:1), we are
urged to uproot ourselves, to be nomads travelling away
from security towards a strange land. Always we are exiles,
journeying towards the homeland which we shall see only
in heaven: as St Paul says, "Our commonwealth is in heaven,
and from it we await a Saviour, the Lord Jesus Christ, who
will change our lowly body to be like his glorious body, by
the power which enables him even to subject all things to
himself" (Phil 3:20-21).

The king will desire our beauty, but only if we take the
trouble to present ourselves before him in humility: "He is
your lord, pay homage to him." There is no place for human
pride in his presence: and even if through Christ we have
the confidence to stand before him, yet we must remember
his words to Moses, "Man may not see me and live" (Exod
33:20). The Fathers continually tell us that the reason
Christ gave us his flesh and blood under the appearances
of bread and wine was that we could not look upon the
naked reality of our God and live: we need the forms of
the sacraments, which simultaneously bring us to God *and*
preserve the distance from him which we need if our
creaturely frailness is not to be swamped by his greatness.

When we come before him, we stand empty-handed —
as Job says, "Now my eye sees you; therefore I despise
myself, and repent in dust and ashes" (42:5-6). But this is
not the whole truth of our situation — if it were, we could
only despair. At the mountain of transfiguration, "the
disciples heard the voice, and fell on their faces, and were
filled with awe. But Jesus came and touched them, saying,
'Rise, and have no fear'" (Mt 17:6-7). When we are con-
fronted by the glory of God, we must fall, as Esther fell
in a faint in the presence of the king; but he raises us up
through his Son, as the king raised up Esther, and tells us,
"Have no fear." And so we find that we are naked, and

yet clothed: "The daughter of the king is clothed with splendour, her robes embroidered with pearls set in gold." We are naked, yet we are clothed. We are empty, yet we are full. We may remember the promise in the visions of Revelation: "I heard a voice from heaven saying, 'Write this: Blessed are the dead who die in the Lord henceforth'. 'Blessed indeed,' says the Spirit, 'that they may rest from their labours, for their deeds follow them!'" (14:13). Those who have laboured in the vineyard of the Lord, and have borne the burden of the day and the heat, will indeed receive from him the denarius which is their reward. But, when they acknowledge his payment of the reward for their hard work, they will also hear him say, in the words of Psalm 80, "*I* relieved your shoulder of the burden; your hands were freed from the basket. In distress you called, and *I* delivered you."

The second part of Psalm 44 continues, "She is led to the king with her maiden companions. They are escorted with gladness and joy; they pass within the palace of the king." We may be reminded by these words that we never stand all alone when we come before God. The salvation brought by Jesus was not something that touched you and me as isolated individuals: it was something that brought you and me into a community. When we stand before the Lord, we stand in the company of our fellow-disciples, of all those others who have heard his voice and have said, "Speak, Lord, your servant is listening." And this is not simply a horizontal community, stretching across the world at this moment: it has a vertical dimension, going backwards and forwards. This is why we can and must pray for the dead, for in the sight of God they are not dead, but are alive; and this is why we can ask the saints to pray for us, just as we can ask each other to pray for us. The communion of saints enables you to pray for me now, but also when I am dead: it enables you to pray for me now, but also when you are dead. And we should not forget to pray for those as yet unborn — they will face problems in following Christ which we cannot imagine, and they too need the support of our intercession.

"They are escorted amid gladness and joy." I have said rather a lot so far about our sin, and while you might perhaps expect that from a Scottish theologian anyway, it could all be rather depressing! There is no good in our forgetting that we are sinners, because if we do, we shall float off on clouds of unreality. And the one door which God cannot batter down is a door of unreality — as long as we have false images of ourselves, we *cannot* respond to his voice. But I have also tried to balance these reflections on our sinfulness by speaking of the reality of grace at work in us. For religion is not meant to be a gloomy thing: Jesus summed up his ministry by saying, "I have spoken these things to you, that my joy may be in you, and that your joy may be full" (Jn 15:11).

"They are escorted amid gladness and joy." The fear of the Lord, which is the beginning of wisdom, is not some abject attitude of quaking and shuddering at the prospect of eternal hellfire if we disobey a tyrant God. No, the fear of God is an aspect of our joy at loving him. Something that we recognise in our love of human beings is surely a kind of fear, a fear of hurting someone we love, and a fear at the prospect that opening ourselves to this other person means that we must make sacrifices of our own inclinations, our own comfort, our own security. For we cannot have love, and security — whether we think of the love of God, or the love of his creatures, love is something infinitely costly. It cost Jesus his life, on the cross; and it will cost *us* no less, if we truly resolve to love him, and to love one another in his Spirit. But this is not something that could ever make us draw back in trembling! If there is indeed something here that we can call "fear", it is the sort of fear of which the Book of Sirach speaks: "The fear of the Lord is glory and exultation, and gladness and a crown of rejoicing. The fear of the Lord delights the heart, and gives gladness and joy and long life" (1:11-12). There is nothing abject there! All the abject fear is expelled by the love of the Lord — as St John says, "There is no fear in love, but perfect love casts out fear. For fear has to do with punishment, and he who fears is not perfected in love. We love, because he first loved us" (1 Jn 4:18-19). And so, although the princess is told to "pay homage" to her Lord, although in herself she has no possible claim on his favour, yet she is led forward, "amid gladness and joy", because in her love she hastens forward, cleansed from the unholy fear which poisons so much of human existence, and cleansed *in* the holy fear which is the beginning of true knowledge and wisdom. The bride in the Song of Songs speaks for us, for you and me and for all of the Church, when she cries out, "O that his left hand were under my head, and that his right hand embraced me!" (2:6). Her love will cost her much pain, much searching — "I sought him, but found him not; I called him, but he gave no answer. The watchmen found me, as they went about in the city; they beat me, they wounded me, they took away my mantle, those watchmen of the walls" (3:1; 5:7) — but she does not give up her search, and eventually she is able to say again, "O that his left hand were under my head, and that his right hand embraced me! . . . Many waters cannot quench love, neither can floods drown it" (8:3,7). "They are escorted amid gladness and joy; they pass within the palace of the king."

"Sons shall be yours in place of your fathers: you will make them princes over all the earth." The princess has given up her father's house and her people, and she is promised in return that she is to be the mother of many princes. Similarly, Abraham was promised that when he left his father's house, "I will make of you a great nation, and I will bless you, and make your name great, so that you will be a blessing" (Gen 12:2). The Fathers love to apply to the Church the words of Isaiah 54, quoted by St Paul in Galatians 4, "Sing, O barren one, who did not bear; break forth into singing and cry aloud, you who have not been in travail! For the children of the desolate one will be more than the children of her that is married, says the Lord." And this theme, that the barren one is to be the mother while she who has children now will be forsaken, is a common one in the scriptures. Let me begin by saying that I think the way in which this theme has been developed in some patristic writing, by declaring that the Church of the Gentiles has received the children while the people of the Jews has been doomed to childlessness, has nothing to commend itself to us today. We have seen too much in this century of the horrors to which anti-semitism has given occasion, to permit us to be happy with that kind of use of scripture. Fulfilment of the Old Testament, as I tried to bring out in the last chapter, does not mean that the Jews have been tossed on to the scrap-heap, or that the Old Testament is worthless unless we allegorise it heavily. Having said that, let me go on to say immediately that the theme of the barren one who bears children is surely immensely rich, especially for those of us who have committed ourselves to live the Christian life in celibacy. Jesus promises that "there is no one who has left house or brothers or sisters or mother or father or *children* or lands, for my sake and for the gospel, who will not receive a hundredfold now in this time, houses and brothers and sisters and mothers and *children* and lands, with persecutions, and in the age to come eternal life" (Mk 10:29-30). This does not mean that a celibate life is in itself a better way of following Christ than a married life — either can be glorious, and either can be squalid. But it does mean that those of us who have heard his call to follow him in celibacy, and who therefore give up the possibility of giving birth to children and bringing them up, are not thereby deprived of the possibility of being fathers and mothers. If we surrender ourselves to Jesus Christ, accepting that that is no empty phrase of sentimental piety, but means a commitment to follow him "with persecutions" as he says, then we shall even now receive back a hundredfold from his bounty, and in the age to come we shall have eternal life.

This is true also of the Church: we call the Church "our holy mother the Church", and there is something more to that than a pious cliché. I spoke in the last chapter of the fact that none of us has invented Christianity for himself — we step into a dance which has already begun without us, and which will go on after we, you and I, have stopped dancing. And it is here that we can indeed see something very positive in the traditional Catholic practice of speaking of the Church as something "out there", something objective which transcends this particular group or that particular group. There is a givenness in our faith, in our worship, in our experience of the Holy Spirit: we are the children of those who went before us, and we in our turn must be the mothers and fathers of those who come after us. Whether we like it or not, we all do in fact play a part in the transmission of the faith to those we know, and to those who will come after us: since this is so, we must constantly purify ourselves so that what is transmitted will contain more and more of Christ and less and less of ourselves. We remember St Paul's image, when he speaks of the various ways in which we can build upon the foundation of Christ, when we transmit the gospel: "Now if any one builds on the foundation with gold, silver, precious stones, wood, hay, straw — each man's work will become manifest, for the Day will disclose it, because it will be revealed with fire, and the fire will test what sort of work each one has done. If the work which any man has built on the foundation survives, he will receive a reward. If any man's work is burned up, he will suffer loss, though he himself will be saved, but only as through fire" (1 Cor 3:12-15). Only as through *fire* — those are terrifying words to hear. But that is equally true in the business of bringing up human children: the Book of Proverbs has loud praise for the good parents who bring up their children well, but there are corresponding warnings for those who fail to reprove their children. Naturally, we as individuals have this responsibility in different ways; but, like the duty to pray, the duty to teach by example and by word is a duty that falls on all of us.

The final verse of the psalm, "May this song make your name for ever remembered. May the peoples praise you from age to age", reminds us of the extension of the community of the faithful through time and space, the extension of which Psalm 86, the praise of Zion, has traditionally been understood to speak. Zion is the mother of all — the promise to the Zion of the old covenant is fulfilled in the Zion of the new covenant, our mother the holy Church which is built on the foundation of the apostles and prophets, with Christ Jesus himself as the corner-stone.

All things come back to Christ, in our reflections on what prayer in the Church means. It is he alone who can speak these words to the princess; it is he alone who can ensure that her name is for ever remembered. If the Church is the spotless bride of the Lamb, that is only because "Christ loved the church and gave himself up for her, that he might sanctify her, having cleansed her by the washing of water with the word, that he might present the church to himself in splendour, without spot or wrinkle or any such thing, that she might be holy and without blemish" (Eph 5:25-27). Always he has the initiative, and "we are to grow up in every way into him who is the head, into Christ" (Eph 4:15). As he says in the fourth gospel, "Apart from me you can do nothing" (15:5).

So we may now consider the first part of Psalm 44, the verses which are addressed by the poet to the king. He too is beautiful: "You are the fairest of the children of men and graciousness is poured upon your lips: because God has blessed you for evermore." An early Christian poet, one of the very earliest of the disciples of Jesus to respond in song to the revelation of the love of God in his Son, says (Odes of Solomon 7:3-4):

> "There is a helper for me, the Lord.
> For he has shown himself to me without grudging in his
>   simplicity,
> for his kindess has diminished his dreadfulness.
> He became like me, that I might receive him".

He could have shown himself to us as a great military commander, but instead he came in a stable at Bethlehem, and washed his disciples' feet. And in all of this, he showed us his beauty — not some empty prettiness, but the beauty of the love that is stronger than death, a beauty that persisted when all his merely human attractiveness was gone on the

cross and "he had no form or comeliness that we should look
at him, and no beauty that we should desire him" (Is 53:2).
The death of Jesus was not *pretty*. But it was indeed something beautiful, for in it the world was remade, and all that
was upside-down was set upright once more.

The words of the poet of Psalm 44, "O mighty one, gird
your sword upon your thigh; in splendour and state, ride on
in triumph for the cause of truth and goodness and right",
emphasise that this beauty of which we speak is not something weak, but a vigorous beauty that carries all before it:
"Your arrows are sharp: peoples fall beneath you." If we
are to understand these verses Christologically, we must
see them in the light of those words about beauty and love:
his triumph, so decisive that it can be described in the
language of victory in war, was a triumph in the hearts of
men. He saw the beauty of the princess and went out to do
battle: she saw his beauty and surrendered to him. His
power is the power of his Father, a power that is utter,
unconditional vulnerability. For, God, who need not have
created men and women, chose to do so; and although he
need not have given us free will, he chose to do so; and
hence he is for ever vulnerable. He calls, and it is up to us
whether or not we answer. He may threaten, but in the
end he has chosen to be vulnerable: he has no pleasure in
the death of a sinner, but rather delights in our repentance,
that we may live. But this vulnerability is not weak! It is
the very exercise of his strength, of his power to woo us in
the sending of his Son, whose beauty must draw us after
him. "He had still one other, a beloved son; finally he sent
him to them, saying, 'They will respect my son'" (Mk 12:6).
Surely it was unthinkable that we could reject this final
messenger? And even when we did reject him, his love was
stronger than death — he raised him from the grave to which
our sins had condemned him, and poured out the Holy
Spirit — all so that we might come in Jesus to the fullness
of life which was the object of our creation. If we do choose
to reject the love of God, we are in fact choosing non-exis-
tence. It is not for us, you and me, to speculate whether in

fact anyone actually *does* reject God's love so decisively as that; what matters for us is not the fear of hell, for ourselves or for anyone else, but the reality of God's voice calling to us, "Harden not your hearts!" He has revealed his love and mercy to us, and it is now for us to respond by taking up the cross and following in the footsteps of our Saviour. And if we do, we shall find that, as Psalm 44 says, our hearts overflow, as we follow him who loved righteousness and hated wickedness, Jesus whom God has anointed with the oil of gladness beyond all others. Always, we meet this paradox that somehow defines our Christian existence: joy in sorrow. We shall never find the joy if we try to insulate ourselves from the sorrow; but if we lay ourselves open in the sort of vulnerability with which God laid himself open to us, then we shall find a genuine peace.

The first part of Psalm 44 ends with the words, "On your right stands the queen in gold of Ophir." These words are clearly a bridge-passage into the second part of the poem, which is addressed to the princess who is to marry the king. But we might briefly consider another aspect of the traditional interpretation of this psalm, that which applies parts of it to Our Lady. What I want to say here will not be distinctively different from other aspects of the interpretation I have been proposing, for it is a general understanding of those who wish to see the Old Testament as speaking of Our Lady that what is said about the Church can be said about her too.

If it is dangerous to see "the Church" as something out there, rather than as you and me, it is also dangerous to separate Our Lady from the rest of us, and view her as something existing in a category all by herself. For she is one of us, flesh of our flesh and bone of our bone, one of the redeemed, who was given by Jesus to the Beloved Disciple to be his mother and so, implicitly, to all of us who are disciples of Jesus. When one member of the Body rejoices, all the body rejoices with it: and so we rejoice at the glorification of Mary because we, her brothers and sisters, share in her glory. "Henceforth all ages will call me blessed", she says in the Magnificat; in her obedience, Eve's disobedience is balanced, and the way is open for Christ the redeemer to come. That is why we read from Genesis 3 in the office for 8 September, the Birthday of Our Lady. The office of the Byzantine rite for that day emphasises another Old Testament theme, applying to Mary a passage from Ezekiel's vision of the new Temple: "Then he brought me back to the outer gate of the sanctuary, which faces east; and it was shut. And he said to me, 'This gate shall remain shut; it shall not be opened, and no one shall enter by it; for the Lord, the God of Israel, has entered by it; therefore it shall remain shut'" (44:1-2). This gate is a symbol of Mary's virginity, as is the fleece of Gideon which was wet when all around it was dry (cf. Judg 6:36ff., and the antiphons at Vespers of 1 January in the Roman Breviary). Likewise, she is the bridalchamber from which Christ the Sun of the world has gone forth to run his course with joy — an image drawn from Psalm 18.

As we apply all these images to Mary, we are not to think that she is separated from us. God made use of ordinary human things in his work of redemption, and the Mother of God was one of us. When she prays for us, she prays as one of us in the mystical Body of her Son. The prayers of the Mother of God are surely very powerful: as the letter of James says, "the prayer of a righteous man has great power in its effects" (5:16). But, whatever power any of our prayers may have is God's gift to us, and his secret until we stand before him in heaven; and devotion to Mary must be firmly rooted in the realisation that she in herself is nothing, she is only the handmaid of the Lord. That is her lowliness — and that is her glory. If we, too, could say with her, *"Ecce ancilla Domini,* be it done to me according to your word," then we too could hear the words of Jesus, "My mother and my brothers are those who hear the word of God and *do* it" (Lk 8:21) — and hear those words, not only as words of judgement, but as words of salvation.

So once more we are pointed firmly back to ourselves — we are asked to change our hearts, and to walk on the path

on which Christ walked. We too must forget our people and
our father's house, just as we might say he forgot all the
dignity that was his as the only-begotten Son of God, and
stripped himself of all that glory so that we might be clothed
in it, so that by his poverty he might make us rich. We too
must strip ourselves of the glory that we think we may have,
and let *him* clothe us. Like Mary, we must be content to
let the Holy Spirit overshadow us: and then, like her, we·
may be led into the presence of the king amid joy and
gladness. Her words to the servants at the wedding feast of
Cana, "Do whatever he tells you" (Jn 2:5), sum up the
whole business of the Christian life. We can have no other
aim than to keep the commandments of Christ: and, if we
do, the water of our weakness will be changed into wine; if
we listen obediently to his voice, the voice that one day
will summon the dead from their graves to judgement, then
we shall find that we too, like the princess of Psalm 44, are
desired by the king. He will look on us, and he will love us:
for, in our faces, he will see his own craftsmanship. Indeed,
he will see more — if you look very closely into the eyes of
another person, you will see the reflection of your own
face. And that is what he will see in us: not simply an
external reflection, but his own image shining out from our
eyes. That is the kind of unity of which·he speaks in his
high-priestly prayer: "that they all may be one: even as you,
Father, are in me, and I in you, that they also may be in us"
(Jn 17:21). Such is his promise to those who love him and
keep his commandments. Such is the promise that we must
have in our minds when we pray the Psalms.

For, while we are still exiles, away from our homeland,
we must sing to keep our courage high, we must comfort
one another with the promises of our Master. "How lovely
is your dwelling place, O Lord of hosts! My soul longs, yea,
faints for the courts of the Lord; my heart and flesh sing
for joy to the living God" (Ps 83:1-2). He sent Paul a thorn
in the flesh, to keep him from being "too elated by the
abundance of revelations" (2 Cor 12:7); and, although he
does indeed give us drink here and now from the torrent of

his delights, although he does indeed feed us with manna as we go through the wilderness of this world, he has planted a thorn in our flesh too, so that we shall always be ill at ease when we are away from him. "My desire is to depart and be with Christ," says Paul, "for that is far better" (Phil 1:23). When we sing in Psalm 44 of the marriage of the king and his bride, when we think of the marriage of Christ and his Church, we must not forget that this is something that is not yet fulfilled. The invitations have been sent out to the wedding feast, but the hall is not yet full. As we wait for his coming, when finally all things will be resolved, and he will reward the servants who have been watching for him, let us keep his promises before our eyes. "If a man loves me he will keep my word, and my Father will love him, and we will come to him and make our home with him" (Jn 14:23). That is true for us even now, even in our brokenness: and that is the pledge of eternal life with him.

For it is in him, in Jesus Christ, that all the longing of the prayer of the Psalms, all the joy, all the confidence, finds its fulfilment — a fulfilment that surpasses all that could ever have been thought of, *excedens omne gaudium et omne desiderium,* surpassing every joy and every desire.

4   The resurrection and the life

"Dying, you destroyed our death: rising, you restored our life." These words of the liturgy proclaim the core of our Christian belief: that Jesus "has abolished death and brought life and immortality to light through the gospel" (2 Tim 1:10). As he says, "I am the resurrection and the life; he who believes in me, though he die, yet shall he live, and whoever lives and believes in me shall never die" (Jn 11:25).

Nothing less would do, if the whole man was to be saved. Physical death may perhaps, in some circumstances, not be the worst thing that could happen to us — arguably, a quick death is to be preferred to injuries that bring long years of suffering. But it is certain that physical death poses the question of the real meaning of our existence with an unrivalled sharpness. As the Book of Job says, "There is hope for a tree, if it be cut down, that it will sprout again, and that its shoots will not cease. Though its root grow old in the earth, and its stump die in the ground, yet at the scent of water it will bud and put forth branches like a young plant. But man dies, and is laid low; man breathes his last, and where is he? As waters fail from a lake, and a river wastes away and dries up, so man lies down and rises not again" (14:7-12). Psalm 29 cries out desperately to God to deliver the singer from the emptiness of death: "What profit is there in my death, if I go down to the dust? Will the dust praise you? Will it tell of your faithfulness? Hear, O Lord, and be gracious to me! O Lord, be my helper!" We find the same anxiety before death in the prayer of King Hezekiah in Isaiah 38: "My dwelling is plucked up and removed from me like a shepherd's tent; like a weaver I have rolled up my life; he cuts me off from

the loom . . . Sheol cannot thank you, death cannot praise
you; those who go down to the pit cannot hope for your
faithfulness."

This attitude to death is not the whole story, of course.
Through the history of the old covenant, we can see signs
of another view of death, which finds its final expression in
the twelfth chapter of the Book of Daniel: "Many of those
who sleep in the dust shall awake, some to everlasting life,
and some to shame and everlasting contempt. And those
who are wise shall shine like the brightness of the firmament;
and those who turn many to righteousness, like the stars
for ever and ever." This belief was not universal among the
Jews in the time of Jesus; as we know, the Sadducees did
not believe that there would be a resurrection, since this
belief could not be proved from the Pentateuch of Moses.
But Jesus himself proclaimed the resurrection in his teaching,
and it was his own resurrection from the tomb that gave
birth to the Church: "If Christ has not been raised," says
St Paul, "your faith is futile and you are still in your sins"
(1 Cor 15:17).

This means that all of the longing of man to be fully
united to his creator, expressed throughout the unfolding
of the old covenant, has now found its answer in the rising
of Jesus from the dead. It is certain that we shall die —
nothing can prevent that. But now that one of us, flesh of
our flesh, has risen from the grave, death has lost its sting.
On Holy Saturday, we place on the lips of Christ at vespers
the words of Hosea, *O mors, ero mors tua,* "O death, I shall
be your death! O Sheol, I shall be your destruction!"
(13:14), because, in his cross and resurrection, he has fulfilled the prophet's hope. He has opened a pathway for us
to walk after him — for the Easter events were not simply
an episode in the private biography of Jesus of Nazareth,
but were an episode in the lives of all men: "for as in Adam
all die, so also in Christ shall all be made alive" (1 Cor
15:22). Jesus, the firstborn from the dead, is the first of
many brothers: where he has gone before us, as head of
the redeemed humanity, we the members of his body, his

brothers and sisters, shall follow, "provided we suffer with him," as Paul tells us, "in order that we may also be glorified with him" (Rom 8:17). "If we have died with him, we shall also live with him; if we endure, we shall also reign with him" (2 Tim 2:11-12).

This truth finds expression in every facet of our lives as disciples of Jesus: it is in dying that we live. If we cling on to our life, we shall lose it eternally – if we let go, we shall find it eternally. This truth only makes sense if we live it! It cannot be demonstrated on some theoretical level, or backed up by philosophical arguments. It can be affirmed only by those who begin to surrender their lives to God, to be remade in the image of his Son who died on the cross, his Son who loved us and gave himself for us. "For this reason the Father loves me," says Jesus, "because I lay down my life, that I may take it again. No one takes it from me, but I lay it down of my own accord" (Jn 10:17-18). For the disciple of such a master, there can be only one path: "where I am, there shall my servant be also" (Jn 12:26).

"There is salvation in no one else", says St Peter in Acts 4:12. This is because only Jesus can offer a salvation that truly gets to grips with man's fundamental need to have life: only Jesus teaches that to have life we must be prepared to lay down our lives, only Jesus shows us that the way to fulfilment lies through a total stripping. Jesus refused the temptation in the garden to ask his Father for twelve legions of angels. He refused the invitation from the chief priests and scribes to come down from the cross so that they could be convinced of his Messiahship. He hung there naked, trusting only in God's righteousness to deliver him. And he was delivered – not like Hezekiah, who was spared for a few years from dying, not like Lazarus, who was raised from the tomb only to die again later; but delivered by being exalted to the right hand of the Father, in the plenitude of absolute life: "Christ being raised from the dead will never die again; death no longer has dominion over him" (Rom 6:9). And such is the pledge he makes to us: "This is the will of my Father, that every one who sees the Son and believes in him should have eternal life; and I will raise him up at the last day . . . he who eats my flesh and drinks my blood has eternal life, and I will raise him up at the last day" (Jn 6:40, 54).

To eat the flesh of Christ and to drink his blood in the eucharist is to renew the commitment of our baptism to die with Christ. We have already passed into eternal life in our baptism, when we were submerged in the waters and rose to be clothed in the white garments which are the vesture of those in paradise; but, looked at from another point of view, we are still pilgrims, who have escaped from Egypt and crossed the Red Sea, but now have a long journey ahead through the desert of this world. And, just as the angel told Elijah in the wilderness, "Arise and eat, else the journey will be too great for you" (1 Kings 19:7), and strengthened him on his way to Horeb the mountain of God, so we in our turn hear the words, "Come, eat of my bread; and drink of the wine I have mixed" (Prov 9:5), in order that we too may not faint or grow weary on our journey to the promised land of heaven. The food of the eucharist is given to us as rations for our journey — for we have not yet arrived in the kingdom, and only when we have will Jesus' promise be fulfilled, "To him who conquers I will grant to eat of the tree of life, which is in the paradise of God" (Rev 2:7). So we are not given now a food which will be completely satisfying, lest we forget that we are only pilgrims. Though our food is the flesh of Christ, and our drink his blood that was shed for us, still we must yearn for the fullness of which this is but the foretaste: "Those who eat me will hunger for more, and those who drink me will thirst for more" (Sir 24:21). Nothing *on earth* can quiet the longings of our hearts, not even the fellowship of the table of the Lord of our hearts; for here we have no abiding city. We have still many mile-posts to pass on our road to the resurrection, and, by eating the body which was broken for us in death and drinking the blood which was poured out for us, we pledge ourselves to follow our Lord in his nakedness, in his uncompromising consecration to do his Father's will, in his readiness to suffer and so — *only* so — to enter into his glory.

We have no powers of our own to draw on. That is something we learn as we go further on the way — initially, we tend to believe that we can get by quite well on our own resources. But, as we progress in the following of Jesus, we learn that our own human resources will not carry us very far — for, as the New Testament reminds us, "we are not contending against flesh and blood, but against the principalities, against the powers, against the world rulers of this present darkness, against the spiritual hosts of wickedness in the heavenly places" (Eph 6:12). In such a conflict, whatever natural strengths of character you and I happen to possess are not likely to be of much use! Jesus tells us that "no one can enter a strong man's house and plunder his goods, unless he first binds the strong man" (Mk 3:27). It is he himself who has bound the strong man and plundered his treasuries: if we want to do the same, we must use the chain that he has forged for us in his victory. And this we can do, if we cast off all reliance on ourselves and say to him, "Make haste to help me, O Lord, my salvation!"

If we do so call to him, he will always answer us, for the Head cannot be indifferent to the sufferings of his body. Paul, on the way to Damascus, heard a voice that asked, "Saul, Saul, why are you persecuting *me*?" (Acts 9:4). Wherever his disciples suffer, there Jesus too suffers — and there, too, he comes to their help. God is a "God who comforts us in all our sorrows" (2 Cor 1:4), a God who acts to save those who trust in him. And so when we pray, "Make haste to help me, O Lord, my salvation!", we pray in the hope that, just as the three young men in Babylon were delivered from the flames of the burning fiery furnace by the presence of a fourth figure "like a son of the gods" (cf. Dan 3), so we too will experience the presence of Jesus as our fellow-sufferer and our deliverer. We must not expect to be whisked off away from the turmoil into a safety-zone, for "all those who desire to live a godly life in Christ Jesus will be persecuted" (2 Tim 3:12), and we have no grounds to ask for a special exemption from this rule of discipleship; but we may indeed hope that in our distress, in the broken-ness of our pain — physical or mental or moral, the pain of martyrdom or temptation or spiritual barrenness and empti-ness — Jesus will be there, according to his promise, "I am with you always, to the close of the age" (Matt 28:20). He will be there. For "neither death, nor life, nor angels, nor principalities, nor things present, nor things to come, nor powers, nor height, nor depth, nor anything else in all creation, will be able to separate us from the love of God in Christ Jesus our Lord" (Rom 8:38-39).

This, as I said earlier, is not some abstract theological notion. It is a fact of our experience as followers of Jesus. We quickly learn the limitations of our own resources: but then we may begin truly to understand something of what his divine resources are. For "every one who calls on the name of the Lord will be saved" (Rom 10:13).

I have twice quoted the words of Psalm 37, "Make haste to help me, O Lord, my salvation!" This is one of the psalms that can be read on several levels. First, it bears the title, "A Psalm of David", and it can be read and prayed taking the words as referring to a literal historical situation in which someone prayed for deliverance. But a richer approach to praying this psalm would be to take the words as, first of all, the words of Jesus to his heavenly Father and, then, our own words as his disciples. To pray the psalm in this way will let us experience in our prayer something of what it *means* to say that Christ is with us when we suffer.

He has taken on himself all of our pain and all of our sin — so he can pray, "There is no soundness in my flesh because of your indignation; there is no health in my bones because of my sin. For my iniquities have gone over my head; they weigh like a burden too heavy for me." He was the one human being whose life was free from sin: yet, as St Paul says, "for our sake, God made him to be sin who knew no sin, that in him we might become the righteousness of

God" (2 Cor 5:21). All the long weariness of our human misery and sin is taken on by Jesus, so that he may truly be "the Lamb of God, who takes away the sin of the world" (Jn 1:29); for our sake, he can say, "I am utterly spent and crushed; I groan because of the tumult of my heart." He was deserted by his closest followers, and so he can say, with the psalmist, "My friends and companions stand aloof from my plague, and my kinsmen stand afar off." With David, with the psalmist, with Jeremiah and all the men of the old covenant who suffered for God, he can say, "Those who seek my life lay their snares, those who seek my hurt speak of ruin, and meditate treachery all day long." And, with the psalmist, Jesus says, "O Lord, you know all my longing: my groans are not hidden from you . . . I count on you, O Lord: it is you, Lord God, who will answer. I pray: 'Do not let them mock me, those who triumph if my foot should slip' . . . O Lord, do not forsake me! My God, do not stay afar off! Make haste to help me, O Lord, my salvation!"

To pray this psalm as the prayer of Jesus is not an easy thing to do. There are two main reasons for this. In the first place, we must realise that it is we *ourselves* who are the enemies! There is not a bit of good in our reading passages of scripture about evildoers and hypocrites, about those "who hold the form of religion but deny its power" (2 Tim 3:5), and thinking that the word of God is speaking about somebody else. It was because of *my* sin and *your* sin that God became man and died on the cross: all human beings stand in the dreadful solidarity of sin, and all of us must hear the word as a word of judgement. So, when we place on the lips of our redeemer a passage like, "Those who render me evil for good are my adversaries because I follow after good", it is ourselves that we are condemning — not some collection of other people, but ourselves. It is ourselves who say, "Let us lie in wait for the righteous man, because he is inconvenient to us and opposes our actions . . . he became to us a reproof of our thoughts; the very sight of him is a burden to us" (cf. Wis 2:12ff.). It is to us, to me

and to you, that he puts the questions, "O my people, what
have I done to you? In what have I wearied you? Answer
me!" (cf. Mic 6:3). None of us is *ever* exempt from these
questions; it is the universal teaching of the Fathers that,
the more deeply we commit ourselves to serve God, the
more deeply we shall find in ourselves the springs of sin,
of ingratitude and bitterness and laziness, of everything
that Jesus came to heal in man. So when we pray Psalm 37,
"Those who are my foes without cause are mighty, and
many are those who hate me wrongfully", and remember
the words of Jesus in the farewell discourses of John, "Now
they have seen and hated both me and my Father. It is to
fulfil the word that is written in their law, 'They hated me
without a cause'" (15:24-25), let us take heed to *ourselves.*
We have no business to condemn anyone else: there is
quite enough sin in any of our own hearts. "If we say we
have no sin, we deceive ourselves, and the truth is not in us.
If we confess our sins, he is faithful and just, and will for-
give our sins and cleanse us from all unrighteousness"
(1 Jn 1:8-9).

The second reason why we find it uncomfortable to pray
Psalm 37 as the prayer of Jesus is because to do so will
bring home to us inescapably the reality of his suffering. If
someone I love is suffering, I cannot remain indifferent —
I suffer too. To meditate on the passion of Jesus, using the
words of the Psalms or of the Book of Lamentations, is a
harrowing experience. The gospel accounts are extremely
sober and restrained. That, of course, is entirely correct,
for the cross is a victory, not a defeat: "He disarmed the
principalities and powers and made a public example of
them, triumphing over them in the cross" (Col 2:15), and
it is the blood shed on the hill of Calvary that brought us
our reconciliation with God and with one another. And we
should certainly not have a morbid interest in the details
of the sufferings of Jesus, gloating over his pain in the
manner of some mystics in the Church's history.

But we should never forget that our freedom from death
was purchased at an enormous price: God "did not spare

his own Son, but gave him up for us all" (Rom 8:32). We see, therefore, the great dignity of man, who was ransomed by the incarnation and death and resurrection of Jesus: we see also the depth of our own sin, which brought such anguish on the Son of God that he could say, in the words of Lamentations, "He drove into my heart the arrows of his quiver; I have become the laughing-stock of all peoples, the burden of their songs all day long. He has filled me with bitterness, he has sated me with wormwood. He has made my teeth grind on gravel" (3:13-16). To meditate on such passages is to realise something of the price of our salvation. "You were bought at a price", Paul tells the Corinthians (1 Cor 6:20). Psalm 37 reveals a little of that price to us: "My heart throbs, my strength fails me; and the light of my eyes — it also has gone from me. My friends and companions stand aloof from my plague, and my kinsmen stand afar off . . ."

Both these considerations — first, that it is we ourselves who are accused in the words of the psalm, and second, that Jesus' love for us led him willingly to such fearsome pain — must lead us to ask ourselves, "If he loved us so much, how are we to respond?" The answer to that is unspectacular, as the Lord told the prophet Micah when he asked, "With what shall I come before the Lord, and bow myself before God on high? Shall I come before him with burnt offerings, with calves a year old? Will the Lord be pleased with thousands of rams, with ten thousands of rivers of oil? Shall I give my firstborn for my transgression, the fruit of my body for the sin of my soul?" (6:6-7). The Lord's answer is, perhaps, disappointingly simple: "He has showed you, O man, what is good; and what does the Lord require of you but to do justice, and to love kindness, and to walk humbly before your God?" That sounds a bit of a let-down after all the marvellous things the prophet proposed to do (all those rivers of oil . . .). Yet, of course, it is its very simplicity that is the difficulty. As St Paul puts it, "If I give away all I have, and if I deliver my body to be burned, but have not love, I gain nothing" (1 Cor 13:3). We

always want to do something flashy for the Lord, when all
he wants is our love: we want to bustle round him like
Martha, when only one thing is needful, to sit at his feet
like Mary. Simplicity, for fallen men and women, is very
difficult to attain — we are prone to a hundred distractions
when we begin to say even a very short prayer like the "Our
Father", and in every one of our activities we find ourselves
wandering far away from the wholeheartedness we should
have.

Only Jesus has ever shown us this singleness of heart, for
it is only in *his* life that God's words to Micah are lived out,
"What does the Lord require of you but to do justice, and
to love kindness, and to walk humbly before your God?"
Only in him does all the fragmentation come together into
a unity of mind and heart and being. Once again, we are
made aware that it is only in Jesus that God hears from
mankind the full response to his summons of love. But
we must also remember that Jesus gave us an example, so
that we would follow where he had walked. We are not
redeemed passively, so to speak; we are redeemed by co-
operating with the graces we receive, by following in the
footsteps of our Master. This is not the result of our own
capabilities, but of his grace acting in us: but, as I pointed
out in the last chapter, God cannot make our response
for us — he woos us, indeed he makes it possible for us to
accept his love and say "yes" to him, but it is up to *us* to
say the "yes".

If we do say "yes" to God, and walk in the footsteps of
Jesus, we open ourselves to the prospect of suffering. Jesus
could not choose the sort of cross he wanted; he was led
away by soldiers. And when he speaks of Peter's death, he
says, "When you are old, you will stretch out your hands,
and another will gird you and carry you where you do not
wish to go" (Jn 21:18). The life of every one of us is a
dialogue between the things we do as subject and the things
other people do to us as object. We cannot choose our own
cross. But we can choose whether that cross is a victory or
a defeat. If Jesus had accepted the challenge to come down

from the cross, it would have been total defeat; and the thief who accepted his punishment on the cross and said to Jesus, "Remember me when you come into your kingdom", was told, "Amen I say to you, today you will be with me in paradise" (Lk 23:40-43). To *accept* suffering is an immensely difficult task, something that seems indeed to fly against the whole instinct for survival which is one of the deepest things in us; but, if we can say, in the words of Psalm 37, "I am like a man who does not hear, and in whose mouth are no rebukes", then we shall be walking on the path of Jesus.

To pray the words of Psalm 37 as Christian disciples is to realise in prayer the truth of what we have been reflecting on: that for the Christian there are no short-cuts to glory, just as for Jesus there was no short-cut to glory. "If any man would come after me, let him deny himself and take up his cross daily and follow me. For whoever would save his life will lose it; and whoever loses his life for my sake, he will save it" (Lk 9:23-24). And it is to realise that we never walk alone: "For you, O Lord, do I wait; it is you, O Lord my God, who will answer", says the psalmist. For he is Immanuel, God with us. If we look to him, as the letter to the Hebrews tells us (12:1-2), we shall conquer and share his throne: but if we look to ourselves, we shall certainly be defeated, as Peter began to sink when he looked, not to Jesus, but to the height of the waves and the force of the gale. But when he cried out to Jesus, "Lord, save me!", "Jesus immediately reached out his hand and caught him . . . and when they got into the boat, the wind ceased" (Matt 14:28ff.).

The reality of our suffering is undeniable: "I am utterly bowed down and prostrate; all the day I go about mourning. For my loins are filled with burning, and there is no soundness in my flesh. I am utterly spent and crushed; I groan because of the tumult of my heart." But if we remember, as we pray these words, that these are also the words of Jesus, and that *he* was heard and rescued, then we can hope for deliverance. Christianity is a religion that can take pain

seriously, and can offer true hope to those who suffer. That
hope is no panacea to wipe out the reality of our suffering,
no narcotic to dull our senses, but the hope given us by the
figure of Jesus on the cross that pain and death do not
have the final word, but that *life* is ultimately triumphant.
The Jesus who tells his disciples to take up their cross and
follow him is also one who promises, "Be faithful unto
death, and I will give you the crown of life" (Rev 2:10).
The great song of the old covenant is, "Give thanks to the
Lord, for he is good; for his steadfast love endures for ever!"
(Ps 135:1). God's love endures beyond the grave, and
wakens the dead to new life, for he has defeated death in
the passion and resurrection of his Son. "Lord, all my
longing is known to you, my sighing is not hidden from
you", says the psalmist; and our God is a God who *acts*.
"Your right hand, O Lord, glorious in power, your right
hand, O Lord, shatters the enemy!" This is the song of
Moses after the crossing of the Red Sea (Ex 15); it is the
song of the baptised after they have conquered in the trials
and temptations of their earthly pilgrimage through the
power of the Holy Spirit. The prayer of Psalm 37 confesses our sins, and calls on God to save us — a call that is
confident. "Wretched man that I am!" exclaims St Paul,
"Who will deliver me from this body of death?" And his
reply is immediate: "Thanks be to God through Jesus Christ
our Lord!" (Rom 7:24-25).

The psalmist in Psalm 37 does not in fact hear the
answer to his pleading. We may perhaps consider briefly
the problem of this kind of prayer that goes apparently
unanswered — a cry for help that seems to be ignored by
God. We are told to pray for what we need, and we are
assured that our prayer is answered by the Father who
loves us: "Ask, and it will be given to you; seek, and you
will find; knock, and the door will be opened to you"
(Lk 11:9). What, then, of the sufferers who pray for relief
and do not find it? What of those who pray for help, and
are left stranded in the barrenness of their souls, who do
not experience anything of the presence of Christ? Is there

anything we can say to such people — indeed, is there anything we can say to ourselves when this is our own experience?

You know the various answers that are given to these questions — that we are not praying hard enough, or not for the right thing, or that God sees that it would be better for us to suffer than to have a cure, or that our suffering is meant to teach us and to enrich us, and so on. It is a problem that darkens the pages of the Book of Job: the conventional religious words of his friends completely fail to accept the *reality* of the challenge that innocent suffering poses to our doctrine and to our experience of a *loving* God. And there is no real answer in the Book of Job itself; Job simply capitulates when God speaks to him, and agrees that he was speaking about things of which he was ignorant. Yet that is *no* solution! The terrible challenge of the fact of innocent suffering remained, and was solved only by Jesus — no intellectual solution (for there is no intellectual solution to the problem of suffering), no neat theological sleight-of-hand that bypasses the problem, but a solution offered in his death. In this death, he shattered all the conventional pieties which we are inclined to utter in the presence of suffering, and for ever showed up their inadequacy.

The only answer to prayer that is unanswered, to love that seems to go to waste like water poured out on sand, to the suffering and grief of the innocent, is given to us by God in the cross. That is his answer. That is his ultimate word to us, his proof to us that he loves and that he suffers in our suffering. As Isaiah says, "In all their affliction he was afflicted" (63:9); though in the life of the Blessed Trinity he exists in unspeakable bliss and does not need his creation, he created us and our world in which we suffer, and he is intimately involved in all that we do, with our joy and with our sorrow. "As a father pities his children, so the Lord pities those who fear him . . . the steadfast love of the Lord is from everlasting to everlasting" (Ps 102:13, 17). And in this love, he held nothing back; he gave us his Son to bring us into the fellowship with him for which he created us, and his Son tasted the bitterness of death so that *we* might taste the freedom of the sons of God.

His Son tasted the bitterness of death. I said earlier that the passion narrative of the gospels is restrained and sober; but no one could ever say that it passes lightly over the reality of Jesus' suffering. His whole ministry, to proclaim the love of God to men and to affirm in his own life that men could fully respond to this love, to declare the nearness of God to his people and the nearness of men to their Father, had been rejected. The religious leaders had plotted against him and brought about his downfall; one of his closest disciples, one of the Twelve, had betrayed him; the others had fled, apart from a tiny band who stood by the cross. And, as he hung on the cross, *he* knew the desolation which *we* all know in our path towards God, the harsh pain of the absence of God, when we can no longer believe, when we can make no emotional response to our intellectual convictions about him, when even we are no longer very sure if we *do* have any intellectual convictions about him, but can only endure: hoping with the mind that he is keeping hold of us, but *feeling* nothing but a heavy deadness of heart. That is a part of our experience, and it was his too.

That final cry, "My God, my God, why have you forsaken me?", is a cry that we all utter at some point. It can be followed by one of two responses to our experience: either we reject the God who seems to be absent when we need him most desperately (and so we become atheists), or else we find ourselves clinging to him with a new depth of love. That is the response of the beloved in the Song of Songs, when finally she finds her lover: "I held him, and would not let him go" (3:4). There are plenty of analogies to this spiritual experience in the experiences of human loving, the love of friends or husband and wife or family: we may find that we come out on the far side of such experiences of darkness with the relationship deepened, or we may find that our fears were justified and so that the relationship is at an end. So with Jesus on the cross: he could have rejected the God who appeared to be powerless to help him, or he could have trusted yet more deeply, yet more hazardously.

Jesus chose to trust — and he came out on the far side of death, raised by his Father to be the first of the new creation; and he poured out the Holy Spirit on his Church so that we, too, could share in this newness. All of our striving, too, is thereby given a new meaning — we are told that, ultimately, nothing is lost, that nothing is in vain, that no prayer is ever forgotten, no suffering ever unhealed. The how and the where and the when of this healing process are God's mystery: he has not revealed that to us. But we are told that no sparrow will fall to the ground without our Father's knowledge (Matt 10:29); and we are told that, at the last, all tears will be wiped away (Is 25:8). When the apostles ask Jesus about the date of the coming of his kingdom, their curiosity is rebuked: "It is not for you to know times or seasons which the Father has fixed by his own authority" (Acts 1:7). Nevertheless, they are promised that "This Jesus, who was taken up from you into heaven, will come in the same way as you saw him go into heaven" (Acts 1:11), and the constant belief of the Church has been that when he comes again all things will be made right.

And so nothing is wasted. Just as the love of Jesus, his fidelity to his ministry of reconciliation between God and men, was not wasted in fact, even though it certainly *seemed* wasted as he hung on the cross, so our love and our suffering are not pointless, even when they seem so. We shall not learn the reasons for this now, for in this life we never hear the full story. But when he comes again, we shall understand fully (cf. 1 Cor 13:12), and we shall see that none of our effort was wasted utterly. When we take the words of Psalm 37 on our lips as the Church's prayer, we pray in the hope of deliverance from our troubles: but, even if that deliverance apparently fails to come, we must not lose our hope. And we must not lose our resolve to be faithful. The three young men in Babylon replied to the king's threats, "O

Nebuchadnezzar, we have no need to answer you in this matter. If it be so, our God whom we serve is able to deliver us from the burning fiery furnace; and he will deliver us out of your hand, O king. *But if not,* be it known to you, O king, that we will not serve your gods or worship the golden image which you have set up" (Dan 3:16-18). "Be faithful unto *death*," says Jesus in the Book of Revelation, "and I will give you the crown of life" (2:10). For some of us, fidelity means a fidelity in the face of a silent and absent God.

"Here indeed we groan", says St Paul (2 Cor 5:2). But he also says, "We *rejoice* in our hope of sharing the glory of God" (Rom 5:2). Our faith is a faith of hopefulness, of watching in joy for the coming of the bridegroom, and in this hope our suffering is to be transfigured. On 26 August 1978, we heard the news of the election of Pope John Paul I. He gave the Church a wonderful testimony to the *joy* of the Christian religion, to the hope which accepts the reality of suffering and sin but accepts the still deeper reality of the love of God, and those of us who lived through those thirty-three days can never forget the joy he radiated, the joy which was a wholly marvellous springtime for the Church. When he died, many people spoke of his "tragically brief" pontificate. Well, it was certainly brief. But was it tragic? No love is ever wasted, no joy is ever lost: the hope John Paul I kindled in the hearts of many, and the pain at his sudden death, are surely also not meaningless, but are a gift of God to spur us on to make the Church ever more deeply what she must be — the community of those who have said "yes" to the love of God, and who are working together in that love to build his kingdom in this world. Was that something "tragic"? On the contrary, it was something glorious.

There is no answer in Psalm 37 to the plea of the psalmist for deliverance from his suffering. But an answer is given in Psalm 21, a psalm which has been interpreted Christologically from the very beginnings of the Christian Church. The opening words were spoken by Jesus on the cross, and the New Testament writers make extensive use of this psalm

when they tell the story of his passion or reflect on its
significance. Like Psalm 37 and the poems of the Book
of Lamentations, this is a psalm which speaks realistically
of the sufferings of the saviour: "I am a worm, and no
man; scorned by men, and despised by the people. All who
see me mock me, they make mouths at me, they wag their
heads; 'He committed his cause to the Lord; let him deliver
him, let him rescue him, for he delights in him!'" But it is
a psalm which is consistently optimistic, which interweaves
the laments with words of confident trust in the Lord:
"Yes, it was you who took me from the womb, entrusted
me to my mother's breast. To you I was committed from
my birth, from my mother's womb you have been my God.
Do not leave me alone in my distress; come close, there is
none else to help." Even though the psalmist is encircled by
his enemies, even though he can count all his bones, still he
trusts that he will be freed from his oppressors, and his trust
is rewarded. The Lord frees him, and he praises his ran-
somer: "For he has not despised or abhorred the affliction
of the afflicted; and he has not hid his face from him, but
has heard, when he cried to him."

Psalm 21 is one of the classic Christological psalms, which
has always been prayed by the Church in the light of the
New Testament; it is also a prayer of the Christian in distress, and a prayer which we can use as a thanksgiving after
we have been set free. It scarcely needs any commentary
from me – let me touch on only two points. First, the
psalmist looks back to the great deeds of God in the past
("In you our fathers put their trust; they trusted and you
set them free. When they cried to you, they escaped. In
you they trusted and never in vain"), and this is the basis
of his confident cry to the Lord, "Save me from the mouth
of the lion, my afflicted soul from the horns of the wild
oxen!" Second, it is a prayer that reflects the missionary
task of the redeemed: the psalmist will proclaim what the
Lord has done for him, and "All the ends of the earth shall
remember and turn to the Lord; and all the families of the
nations shall worship before him . . . posterity shall serve

him; men shall tell of the Lord to the coming generation, and proclaim his deliverance to a people yet unborn, that he has done it." We too look to the past, to the ministry of Jesus which set us free; we too must proclaim this to the world, so that all the nations will come to acknowledge him whom Simeon acclaimed as the light of the Gentiles.

"Dying, you destroyed our death: rising, you restored our life." "We know that we have passed out of death into life", says the first letter of John (3:14), for in Jesus we come to see that darkness cannot quench the light. In the liturgy of the Easter vigil, the paschal candle is lit from the new fire, and then each of our candles is lit from this candle as it is borne through the dark church. So with our life in Christ: he lights up the darkness as he goes ahead of us through this world, and his light is passed on to us so that we, too, may be "light in the Lord" (Eph 5:8). As the liturgy of the dead says, in Jesus *spes beatae resurrectionis effulsit,* "the hope of a blessed resurrection has shone forth". We live in the light of that hope, and we die in the light of that hope.

5   A broken and contrite heart

"Let the word of Christ dwell in you richly, teach and
admonish one another in all wisdom, and sing psalms and
hymns and spiritual songs with thankfulness in your hearts
to God. And whatever you do, in word or deed, do everything in the name of the Lord Jesus, giving thanks to God
the Father through him." These words from the letter to
the Colossians (3:16-17) give us something of a programme
for life in the Body of Christ, a life that is called into existence by the word of Christ to which we respond by our
common worship. It is not our private prayer that comes
first into view, but our liturgical prayer. This shared praise
of God manifests the unity of the faithful, and itself creates
and nourishes the unity it manifests, in such a way that the
Second Vatican Council can speak of the liturgy as the
fons et culmen of all Christian activity, the source of all
we do and the summit towards which all our work is directed
(cf. Constitution on Liturgy, 10). We were created by the
Father so that we might find the fulfilment of our being in
praising his goodness; when we failed to be content with
this, and sought other goals which were false to our nature,
he sent the Son to us, so that, in the words of the Council,
he might "bring to this earthly exile that hymn which is
sung throughout all ages in the heavenly dwellings" (*ibid.,*
83). We have been set free from our dumbness: Jesus has
said "Ephphatha!" to us and unbound our tongues, so
that we, too, may take our part in the liturgy of praise
which is a foreshadowing of the glory of the kingdom of
heaven.

The old covenant contained detailed regulations to safe-
guard the purity of the priests who ministered before the

Lord. Although the death and resurrection of Jesus have
opened a new way for us to the throne of mercy, and
such detailed cultic regulations are for ever superseded, it
remains true that "our God is a consuming fire" (Deut
4:24 and Heb 12:29) and that we who would draw near
to him must be prepared to be purified. When artists
represent the scene of Pentecost from Acts 2, they tend
to show small flames hovering above the heads of the apostles
and Our Lady in the upper room — but the Holy Spirit is
surely more than a small flame. He is a fire, which will burn
up all the chaff; he is the force of love that is strong as
death and sweeps aside all obstacles in its path. The hymn
from the Mass of Pentecost, the *Veni, Sancte Spiritus,*
addresses the Holy Spirit by many gentle and consoling
names, but also prays: *Flecte quod est rigidum, fove quod
est frigidum, rege quod est devium,* "Bend what is stiff,
melt what is frozen, bring order to what is astray." To have
the new life of the Spirit, we must first die to the old Adam
in us, and that is no easy contest. It is a contest which only
the Spirit can win; of ourselves, we are nothing. *Sine tuo
numine, nihil est in homine, nihil est innoxium,* "Without
your divine presence, there is nothing at all in man that is
harmless." But with him, no doors are locked before us.
When Moses consecrated Aaron and his sons to be priests,
he began by washing them with water (cf. Exod 29:4):
when we, the priestly people of the new and eternal covenant, begin to take our responsibilities as priests seriously,
we too must be purified by the Holy Spirit. "Purge me with
hyssop, and I shall be clean", says the psalmist, "wash me,
and I shall be whiter than snow."

These words are taken from Psalm 50, the great psalm
of repentance which occurs again and again in the liturgical
prayer of the eastern Churches, and has a daily place in the
traditional form of the divine office of the Benedictines. Its
title in the Hebrew Bible is, "A Psalm of David, when Nathan
the prophet came to him, after he had gone in to Bathsheba".
The sin of David against Uriah the Hittite, recorded in 2
Sam 11-12, is noteworthy for at least one very interesting

reason: that David did not realise he had sinned in arranging for Uriah to be killed in battle against the Ammonites so that he could marry Bathsheba. When Nathan told him his parable, David was highly indignant, as befitted the king who had to execute judgement for his people: "David's anger was kindled greatly against the man; and he said to Nathan, 'As the Lord lives, the man who has done this deserves to die; and he shall restore the lamb fourfold, because he did this thing, and because he had no pity.'" Nathan's reply is simple: "You are the man." And when the prophet has pronounced God's judgement on the king, David acknowledges, "I have sinned against the Lord." To this, Nathan replies, "The Lord also has put away your sin; you shall not die." When David confesses his guilt, he is forgiven.

The first thing we have to bear in mind as we pray Psalm 50 is, then, that it is a prayer of repentance for a sin which was committed ignorantly. David was so intent on his own interests that he failed to apply to himself the same moral standards that he applied to other people. This is something we do all the time — we are endlessly ready to find excuses for ourselves, and endlessly ready to criticise other people, and it is to *us* that Jesus says, "Why do you see the speck that is in your brother's eye, but do not notice the log that is in your own eye?" As if that were not bad enough, we attempt to set ourselves up as teachers: "Or how can you say to your brother, 'Let me take the speck out of your eye', when there is the log in your own eye?" (Matt 7:3-4). There is indeed a ministry of Christian rebuke, which was mentioned in the passage from Colossians with which I began this chapter, — "teach and admonish one another in all wisdom" — and we must not be so scared of exercising judgement that we keep silent in the presence of grave sin. If I know that someone is being ill-treated and do absolutely nothing about it, then I will hear the words of Jesus, "I was hungry and you gave me no food, I was thirsty and you gave me no drink" (Matt 25:42). But this ministry of Christian rebuke, if it is to be an authentic building-up of the

Body of Christ, must proceed from what Psalm 50 calls
"a broken and contrite heart". It is a ministry which
demands humility for its effective exercise, the humility
of a repentant sinner who invites another sinner to accept
the Father's forgiveness. As St Paul says, "Brethren, if a
man is overtaken in any trespass, you who are spiritual
should restore him in a spirit of gentleness. Look to yourself, lest you too be tempted. Bear one another's burdens,
and so fulfil the law of Christ" (Gal 6:1-2).

"Look to yourself, lest you too be tempted": we must,
therefore, be constantly alert, lest we condemn other people
for doing the same things we excuse in ourselves. It is a use-
less exercise to pray words like, "I know my transgressions,
and my sin is ever before me", when we are sailing ahead
like David, completely wrapped up in ourselves and unaware
that we are sinning. If, however, we think about the words
we are saying, we find that we are committing ourselves to
a radical remaking by God: "Indeed you love truth in the
heart; then in the secret of my heart teach me wisdom . . .
a pure heart create for me, O God, put a steadfast spirit
within me." If we really *mean* what we are saying (and we
ought not to waste God's time and our own by praying for
things we do not want), then we are taking the risk of love.

Part of the risk in human love is that I will give myself
to someone who will not return the love to me. If I open
myself to God, clearly it makes no sense to say that there
is a risk of his rejecting me! He *is* love, as St John tells us;
and, as the Book of Wisdom says, "How would anything
have endured if you had not willed it? Or how would anything not called forth by you have been preserved? You
spare all things, for they are yours, O Lord who love the
living" (11:25-26). If I am able to love God, it is only
because he has first awakened me to life, and has put into
my heart the seed of love for him. Human affections may
fail, but he cannot desert his children: "My father and my
mother have forsaken me," we read in Psalm 26, "but the
Lord will take me up." Surely, then, there is nothing to
fear here?

That all makes excellent sense theologically. But it does
not remove the element of risk from our spiritual lives. For
the risk in our love for God is fundamentally the same as
the risk in our love for his creatures — the risk of dying in
order to live, of losing myself in order to find myself again,
newly made whole, as the gift of another. We hug our
imagined autonomy close to ourselves, and will not understand that to be truly free we must be servants of someone
other than ourselves — it may be a religious community that
asks this surrender of me, it may be my partner in marriage,
it may be the availability to all that shapes the life of a
celibate; it may perhaps take different forms at different
periods of my life. But, always, our lives are lived in interac-
tion with other people who make claims upon us; even a
hermit is not cut off from membership in the mystical
Body of Christ — his life, too, must be shaped by love for
his fellow Christians, if it is to be of any worth. Letting
go of myself in love, whatever precise relationship this
entails with the other or others, is always painful, for it
requires me to yield myself without reserve. But if I do
yield myself, and insofar as I yield myself, in this way, I
shall receive myself back, and I shall breathe life into the
other person whom I love and who loves me. True love is
the ultimate risk, and it is a risk that will never be neutralised
for me as long as I remain open to give and to receive.

If that is our human experience, then how much greater
must the risk be when I surrender myself to *God!* In all
sorts of ways, I can present a false personality to my fellow
creatures in my dealings with them; the progress of many
relationships is the business of getting below the roles we
are playing and having the humility to let ourselves be seen
as we really are, warts and all. It is precisely the same in our
relationship with God: except, that we cannot deceive him
who is the Truth. We are told that Jesus "knew all men and
needed no one to bear witness of man; for he himself knew
what was in man" (Jn 2:25). When we present ourselves to
God, we are not supplying him with information about
ourselves which he did not previously have. He knows what

is in us — and still he loves us, for "we are his workmanship" (Eph 2:10). The Pharisee presented God with a long list of things he was doing, "I fast twice a week, I give tithes of all that I get", and so on: the publican simply "beat his breast, saying, 'God, be merciful to me a sinner!'" And it was the publican who "went down to his house justified" (cf. Lk 18:9ff.). He did not trouble to inform God about himself; he was aware that God knew him, and he was aware that he needed to repent, not to pat himself on the back. If we can take the risk of exposing our wounds to the physician, he will heal them; but he is greatly hampered if we insist that we are not really sick, but are enjoying excellent health. Whatever good may be in us is his gift to us, and we can claim no credit for it; we must thank him for it, but we must not thank *ourselves*! When we look to ourselves, we can say only, "We are unworthy servants" (cf. Lk 17:10).

So we must take the risk of dying, of being burned up in the flame of the Spirit of God. "You have *not* come to what may be touched", the letter to the Hebrews warns us (12:18) — we have come to the incalculable forces of the love of God, and, if we wish to be authentically ourselves in freedom, we must die. That dying is, as we all know, something that will go on as long as we live, for the part of us that is afraid to say "yes" to God is very strong, and continually finds new areas of our life where it can put up the barricades. St John tells us that "perfect love casts out fear" (1 Jn 4:18); but when we are speaking of *this* particular fear, not the fear of rejection, nor the fear of eternal hellfire if we sin, but the fear of dying to self, then we must recognise that "perfect fear" can also cast out love. God can approach us, but he cannot make our response for us: he stands at the door and knocks, but it is *our* job to open. Always throughout our life, he will knock: always, we have to quell our anxieties and open the door to him. That may be a difficult thing to do. But *only* by dying, as Jesus died to his own will in Gethsemane, can we save ourselves. "He who would save his life must lose it" (Mk 8:35).

The prayer of Psalm 50 is a prayer for this fundamental

remaking: "A pure heart create for me, O God . . . a humbled, contrite heart you will not spurn." For the Bible, the heart is the symbol of all that is fundamental in man. When God promises to give a new covenant to replace the bond that his people have rejected, he says, "I will put my law within them, and I will write it upon their hearts; and I will be their God, and they shall be my people" (Jer 31:33). Similarly, when he promises to restore Israel, he says, "I will sprinkle clean water upon you, and you shall be clean from all your uncleannesses, and from all your idols I will cleanse you. A new heart I will give you, and a new spirit I will put within you; and I will take out of your flesh the heart of stone and give you a heart of flesh" (Ezek 36:25-26). Much of the metaphorical language we use in our culture about "love" and "the heart" can lead us to a comfortably sentimental picture of what this involves. But it is not the transfer of some superficial emotion from an idol to the living God: it involves a "broken and contrite heart", a person who has faced up to the radical falseness of his life and has been converted as a *whole* person to the new life; it involves death and rebirth. First we must learn to pray, "Wash me more and more from my guilt, and cleanse me from my sin!" Then we must undergo his searching purification: "Who can endure the day of his coming, and who can stand when he appears? For he is like a refiner's fire and like fuller's soap" (Mal 3:2). He must break us before he can heal us.

But he breaks us only so that he may heal us — he has no delight in our pain or our dying, but rejoices to see us made whole. "Make me hear rejoicing and gladness," says Psalm 50, "that the bones you have crushed may revive . . . give me again the joy of your help." If I have emphasised the difficulty, the arduousness of our dying, let me not omit to emphasise the glory of the healing which we come even now to know. "O Lord, open my lips, and my mouth shall declare your praise!" Our fellowship with God is not an unrelieved climb uphill: "O Lord, how precious is your love. My God, the sons of men find refuge in the shelter of

your wings. They feast on the riches of your house; they
drink from the stream of your delight. In you is the source
of life and in your light we see light." The experience of
the sweetness of the Lord, which prompted the poet to
write Psalm 35, is no less a part of our life with God than the
profound sense of our sin and our need for repentance
which prompted the writing of Psalm 50. Our spiritual
life is indeed something of a dialogue between the two —
because if we sit all day long and contemplate our own
sinfulness and helplessness, we shall end up in despair, while
if we think only of the delights of the love of God, we shall
forget that there is still much in us that has imperfectly
responded to that love. We are redeemed, and we are
sinners. Both are true, and we must not overlook either
pole of this mystery. A gloomy preoccupation with sin is a
profoundly un-Christian state; a gladness that ignores our
poverty before God is an insubstantial state that is equally
un-Christian. A normal Christian (and that is what we all
ought to aim to be!) can always find reasons to thank God,
and reasons to confess.

When we have confessed and been set free from our sin,
then we must proclaim to others what the Lord has done:
"Give me again the joy of your help . . . that I may teach
transgressors your ways and sinners may return to you. O
rescue me, God, my helper, and my tongue shall ring out
your goodness." Our missionary proclamation, as we
reflected at the end of the last chapter, always begins
with the narrative of what the Lord has done — and on the
basis of what he has done in the past, we affirm our hope
in his future acts. It is because I can say, "I sought the Lord,
and he answered me", that I can invite others, "Glorify the
Lord with me, together let us praise his name!" (cf. Ps 33).
The ministry to sinners, to call them back to the Lord, is
based on the same principle. Because this is a Lord who
welcomed me after I had squandered all my inheritance in a
far country, I can invite the others who are far from home
to come back to him. We are not inviting people to join a
group who are convinced of the theoretical soundness

of some concept of personal wholeness: we, who have
acknowledged our sin and have been forgiven by God
through his Son Jesus of Nazareth, and have tasted the
joy of the Holy Spirit, are inviting people to share our
experience. We do not issue our invitation from a position
of superiority, for we know "that the transcendent power
belongs to God, and not to us" (cf. 2 Cor 4:7). And so
we can look forward to the fashioning in Christ of a new
human order: "In your goodness, show favour to Zion:
rebuild the walls of Jerusalem." And this is an order in
which men and women will find their true fulfilment in the
praise of their maker: "Then you will be pleased with law-
ful sacrifice."

When David confessed his sin and received forgiveness,
God blessed his marriage to Bathsheba and gave them a son,
Solomon. When we confess our sin and receive forgiveness,
God heals what was sinful in us and blesses us — so that
we can affirm, in the most awesome paradox of all, that the
sin of Adam, our basic turning-away from God, was a *felix
culpa*, a "happy fault" that won for us the coming of Jesus
to redeem us. As the prayer of the liturgy declares, our
creation was marvellous, but our re-creation in Christ was
yet more marvellous; and we can affirm from our own
spiritual lives that the forgiveness of our sin, the mending
of our brokenness, is the most wonderful of all the manifestations of God's love. He gives us back ourselves, recog-
nisably you and me, but now transfigured in the light that
flows from him. He has given us a new heart, and put a new
spirit within us.

The effect of this new creation in Christ, of this crossing
from death to life, is that we join the community of those
who sing the praise of God. The prayer of Psalm 50, "Have
mercy on me, God, in your kindness. In your compassion
blot out my offence", is not only the prayer of the individual Christian, but also the prayer of the whole Church.
For the Church is redeemed, she is the spotless bride of the
Lamb, "clothed with fine linen, bright and pure" (Rev
19:8): and the Church is also a sinful community in constant

need of repentance. *Nigra sum sed formosa,* "I am very
dark but comely", says the bride in the Song of Songs
(1:5). The Church here on earth will always be both "very
dark" and "comely", always in the process of construction
upon Christ her corner-stone, beautified by his grace and
disfigured by our sin. We could conceivably say to ourselves,
"Well, there will always be sinners — the poor are always
with us", and busy ourselves only about our private salvation. But, since we are members one of another, we must
have a profound concern for the salvation of all who are
in the Church. "The parts that seem to be weaker are indis-
pensable", says St Paul (1 Cor 12:22): there are no first-
class and second-class compartments on the journey to the
heavenly Jerusalem, but we all stand or fall together. "If
one member suffers, all suffer together; if one member is
honoured, all rejoice together" (1 Cor 12:26). This means
that, when we confess our sins in the words of Psalm 50,
we must be aware that in our sinning we not only offend
God and hurt ourselves — we hurt our fellow Christians also.
David's sin was not a purely private affair — it had public
effects, and God threatened to punish him publicly: "You
did it secretly; but *I* will do this thing before all Israel, and
before the sun" (2 Sam 12:12). St Paul tells us that we do
not belong to ourselves, but to Christ who has bought us in
his blood (cf. 1 Cor 6:20): and this means that we belong
to one another. "None of us lives to himself, and none of
us dies to himself . . . let us then pursue what makes for
peace and for mutual upbuilding" (Rom 14:7, 19).

The prayer of the Psalms of repentance is a constant
reminder of our need for examination of conscience, to see
whether the way we live in the fellowship of the Church
is a support or a hindrance to our brothers and sisters. This
is true of prayer by an individual, as for example in the cases
of most of the priests of the Catholic Church, who very
seldom celebrate the divine office in common. But it is
much more effectively true in the case of the prayer of
the psalms by a community. The prayer of a community,
as we reflected earlier, manifests and nurtures the very

being of the Church as a people bound together by their praise of God.

"Two are better than one, because they have a good reward for their toil", says the Book of Ecclesiastes. "For if they fall, one will lift up his fellow; but woe to him who is alone when he falls and has not another to lift him up ... And though a man might prevail against one who is alone, two will withstand him. A threefold cord is not quickly broken" (4:9-12). This passage has played its part in the polemic of monastic writers against the hermit's vocation: they warned that a hermit would have no opportunity to practise fraternal charity, nor to be supported and rebuked by his brethren. We can look at the hermit rather more positively than that, remembering the principle of St Benedict: that no one should attempt the eremitical life until he has been tested by years in community life, and reflecting that the only motive for the hermit must be his burning love for all others. We can then give thanks for this rare vocation in the Church, and, bypassing these negative interpretations of the words of Ecclesiastes, reflect briefly on their relevance to our life of prayer.

There is, clearly, an element of inescapable individuality in our life of prayer. God calls each one of us by name, and loves us, not with a sweeping philanthropic affection for "mankind", but with a father's love for each of his children. "Can a woman forget her sucking child," he asks in Isaiah, "that she should have no compassion on the son of her womb? Even these may forget, yet I will not forget you. Behold, I have graven you on the palms of my hands" (49:15-16). Nevertheless, an unchecked individualism is not the mark of a mature person, but of an infant: "none of us lives to himself." "Woe to him who is alone when he falls and has not another to lift him up", says Ecclesiastes. God has created us in such a way that we minister to one another. "It is not good for the man to be alone," he says in Genesis, "I will make him a helper fit for him" (2:18). Many other words might have been chosen, but here Eve is described quite simply as a "helper": the first human society, in the understanding of this creation narrative, is a harmonius cooperation of man and woman in obedience to God. But, from the outset, this plan was frustrated, when Cain killed Abel — and the catalogue of discord and bloodshed grows ever longer. But in Jesus, men are given again the possibility of living together in harmony. The sacrifice of his death is the culmination of all human sins — there will be nothing worse in all the centuries to come, just as there had been nothing worse in all the centuries of the old covenant. But the cross is not a defeat for God's loving purposes, but a victory: and so the interweaving sins of men do not have the last word. It is now possible for us to live harmoniously together, serving our creator in the freedom of sons and daughters. That possibility is to be realised in the Church.

When we pray together, we must minister to one another, supporting each other in love. The Holy Spirit apportions his gifts variously, and we must not each try to do everything, but must learn to be served, as well as to serve. We all tend to be preoccupied with ourselves: whether it is my tendency to push myself forward aggressively, or to shrink back and protest loudly that I have no abilities, my order of priorities is definitely "myself first". The snare is all the more deadly because it is a question of how we may best serve other people in the community! Self in us is something extremely tenacious, and, like David, who sinned without really noticing what he was doing, we can find that all our efforts to help others have been more basically efforts to promote our own personalities. We are not talking about grave sin here; but when we speak about our progress towards God, our opening ourselves to his grace at work in us to purify us, we shall find, time and again, that the profoundest obstacles are not grave sins (for most of us lead the kind of lives in which there are no occasions of such sins — nuns rarely murder their prioress), but deeply-rooted turns of selfishness and fear and greed in us. These are much harder to tackle than lurid public sins, because of the depth of their roots. And we must never be content to say, "Oh well, God can make use of me even in spite of my sinfulness", and to quote Joseph's words to his brothers in Egypt, "It was not you who sent me here, but God . . . as for you, you meant evil against me; but God meant it for good, to bring it about that many people should be kept alive, as they are today" (Gen 45:8; 50:20), and apply these mysterious words cheerfully to ourselves. It was the Pharisees, the religious people, the good people — not notorious sinners, but men who gave alms and fasted and prayed — who were the most severely condemned by Jesus, and we too must be careful lest we fall under this condemnation.

Prayer in common, especially the prayer of the psalms in the divine office, acts as a mirror in which we may see ourselves, both as individuals and as a community before God. You can always tell a good marriage, partly because of all sorts of minute unconscious signals the partners transmit to each other and to you; and you can normally judge the health of a religious community by participating in its common prayer — whether that is the celebration of Mass in a parish church, or the office in a religious order, or the shared worship of a prayer-group. We can deceive ourselves and others for short periods; but if there is any measure of openness at all in us to the love of God, he will unfailingly reveal to us the shortcomings that others may more easily see. Our failings and our strengths "cannot remain hidden" indefinitely (cf. 1 Tim 5:24-25). When we pray together, then, and confess our sin and offer thanksgiving to God, we come to learn things about ourselves. Am I irritated by the habit of someone who always joins in the responses a couple of syllables later than everyone else? Am I anxious to let my beautiful voice be heard clearly when we sing? Am I intent on moving the worshippers to admire my abilities as a reader, rather than on moving them to conversion by the word of God? Do I find persistently that I have reached the "Glory be to the Father" at the end of psalms without having paid any attention to the words I have just taken on my lips? The tradition of the Fathers rightly emphasises that prayer in common is a unique testing-ground of our spiritual lives. And if you are inclined to object, "These things you have mentioned are just ordinary human reactions — they are not very serious, and anyway they are unavoidable", the answer must be, "We claim to be something more than just ordinary human beings: we claim that we have been redeemed and awakened by Jesus. If we are truly awake, then we must be alert to what we are doing, and to the opportunities for growth which we miss." God accepts us as we are, indeed, and we cannot come before him as anyone other than ourself. But he accepts us in order that he may transfigure us, not so that he may have a Church composed of second-rate Christians. He calls us all to be saints, and saints are people who know what they are doing! "I slept, but my heart was awake", says the bride in the Song of Songs (5:2); the biography of our Christian life is the story of the chasing of our drowsiness, so that we may become totally alert to what God requires of us. "Awake, O sleeper, and arise from the dead, and Christ shall give you light!" These words in Ephesians 5:14 are probably quoted from a hymn addressed to the newly-baptised, but they are addressed by the author of the epistle to *all* Christians, to all who are children of light.

"Behold, how good and pleasant it is when brothers dwell in unity!" exclaims Psalm 132. That unity is something for which we have to pray and strive. If we do not nourish our physical bodies, they will be dissolved in death: if we do not nourish the mystical Body of Christ, it too will be dissolved. And the primary means of nourishing the unity of the Church, as I said in an earlier chapter, is prayer. Insofar as you and I, and all of us as a community, make ourselves over to God to be transformed by him into the likeness of his Son, in a prayer that is the response of our whole being to his love, then brothers will dwell in unity. You will remember the image of the circle and the radii which I quoted: as we draw nearer to him, we draw nearer to each other. The eucharist is the bond that unites us to Jesus: it is also the bond that unites us to one another, and

to the whole of the Church throughout time and space.
When I receive absolution for my sins in the sacrament of
reconciliation, I am made one with God — and I am made
one with the whole of the Christian community, which I
have harmed by my sin. There can be no motive for envy
in the Church: for whatever gifts the Holy Spirit has given
to anyone else are given for *my* benefit. There is no reason
for me to think I am ignored by God because I have not
received his more spectacular charisms; St Paul was knocked
off his horse on the Damascus Road, but, for most of us,
conversion to the Lord and growth in his grace are essentially matters of our everyday living. What we are called by
him to do is to change the structures of our everyday living
in such a way that they become positive channels of his
grace — he *can* work in spite of us, but he prefers to work
through us!

The *perfect* worshipping community, in which everyone
truly helps the others to grow in the grace and knowledge
of the Lord, has never existed: here we are *in via,* not
yet *in patria* where the worship of the saints before the
throne of the Lamb *is* the perfect expression of what they
are by his grace. And so we must strive continually, in a
spirit of repentance, of humility, and of thanksgiving, to
widen our hearts. The Book of Sirach tells us, "The compassion of a man is for his neighbour, but the compassion
of the Lord is for all living beings" (18:13). We are called
to "walk in love, as Christ loved us" (Eph 5:2), to grow
towards the "compassion for all living beings" which the
Father showed us by sending his Son to share our toil and
lowliness. If we dare to sing, "Behold, how good and
pleasant it is when brothers dwell in unity!", when we
know that we have not yet achieved this oneness of heart
in the Lord; if we dare to sing, "My sacrifice is a contrite
spirit. A humbled, contrite heart you will not spurn", when
we know that we are toughly resisting the attempts of the
Holy Spirit to break us and heal us: our boldness can be
justified only by our confidence that our God is a God who
will act, who will answer our cries for help. "Some boast of

chariots, and some of horses," says Psalm 19, "but we boast
of the name of the Lord our God. They will collapse and
fall; but we shall rise and stand upright." Psalm 19 is a
prayer for the king's victory in battle: a prayer, on our
lips, that Christ who conquered sin and death will make us
sharers in his victory. And Psalm 20, the prayer of thanksgiving for victory gained, is likewise, on our lips, a proclamation of joy at the resurrection of Jesus which has
made all things new: "He asked you for life and this you
have given, days that will last from age to age." All of our
prayer is made on the far shore of the river of death, which
Jesus has crossed for us — we call to him in the firm belief
that he will bring us help.

I began this chapter by quoting the words of the letter
to the Colossians, "Let the word of Christ dwell in you
richly, teach and admonish one another in all wisdom, and
sing psalms and hymns and spiritual songs with thankfulness
in your hearts to God. And whatever you do, in word or
deed, do everything in the name of the Lord Jesus, giving
thanks to God the Father through him" (3:16-17). My
reflections on Psalm 50 have been something of a commentary on these verses, and I should like to end now by medi-
tating on the first words, "Let the word of Christ dwell in
you richly".

There is a danger in what I have been saying that we shall
look on the spiritual life as something that consists only of
vigorous struggles and pitched battles; a danger that we
shall concentrate too hard on the passage where St Paul
compares us to athletes competing at the races (1 Cor
9:24ff.). But an essential aspect of the spiritual life is that it
is *God* who is active. And although most of us do need a
good prod every so often, to stop us from falling asleep,
most of us also have a profound need for peace. We have
fallen into the hands of robbers, who have beaten us and
left us half dead, and we need the Good Samaritan to come
and bind up our wounds. God is a God who "heals the
broken-hearted, and binds up their wounds" (Ps 146:3), a
God who revealed himself to Elijah, not in wind nor in

earthquake nor in fire, but in "a still small voice" (1 Kings 19:9ff.). The wind and the earthquake and the fire are part of our experience of God, because our sinfulness makes us deaf to the "still small voice": but when Jesus says "Ephphatha!" to us, he unstops our ears, so that we may hear the voice of the bridegroom. And then he whispers in our ear, "Arise, my love, my fair one, and come away; for lo, the winter is past, the rain is over and gone. The flowers appear on the earth, the time of singing has come . . ." (Song 2:10-12). "For he is our peace", says the letter to the Ephesians (2:14); in him, the war and the bitterness and the fear are stilled, so that our scars may be healed. It is he who fights our battles for us, it is he who brings the victory.

And so we must let his word dwell in us. He calls to us, and we must listen to his voice. We are not told that Mary asked any questions as she sat at Jesus' feet: she just sat there "and listened to his teaching" (Lk 10:39). This is what we must do when we read the scriptures — we must sit at his feet and hear what it is he will say to us. In the prayer of the Psalms, we hear his word addressed to us, and we return it to him in our prayer. "Take with you words and return to the Lord", says the prophet Hosea (14:2): what better words than the words which he has given us, the words of God's Son during his earthly pilgrimage, the words of all who have gone before us in the tradition of the Church? Here too, as in every area of our spiritual life, our power is not our own, but is his gift to us: we were dumb, but he gave us the words to praise him, the words to sing in his presence, the words to confess our sin and to thank him for his forgiveness. His words must ring through our whole being, and set up an echo that will never die away until we stand before his throne and join in the praise of the saints in paradise. For in this way the word of God will be our full nourishment, both in receiving it as his gift to us and in giving it back to him in prayer. The genius of the western Christian tradition has been to fashion a liturgy and a divine office that speak God's own words to him in this way, with a power to strike very deep roots in the hearts of the worshippers. For we are not reading the scriptures now for any secondary reason of our own, such as purposes of academic enquiry, or for weapons in our Christian warfare, or for our private spiritual edification; no, we read the scriptures now because our prayer is truly the voice of the bride as she says to her bridegroom, "Come, Lord Jesus!"

So we shall find that we "do everything in the name of the Lord Jesus, giving thanks to God the Father through him". And so we shall find that truly "he is our peace", a peace not such as the world gives, but the peace of rest eternal. "Be of good cheer", says Jesus to his disciples, "I have overcome the world."

6   The holy of holies

I have kept Psalm 121 until the end of this book, partly
because it is my favourite psalm and I do believe in keeping
the good wine till the last, and partly because its theme is
the culmination of our reflections. "I rejoiced when I heard
them say: 'Let us go to God's house'!" This psalm is a pilgrims' song — to appreciate it, you have to picture a band
of pilgrims making their way up to worship at the Temple
in Jerusalem, and finally arriving: "And now our feet are
standing within your gates, O Jerusalem!" they cry in
excitement. And our journey towards God finds its culmination when we enter his Temple, when we take our places
before his throne in the heavenly Jerusalem, the city that
"has no need of sun or moon to shine upon it, for the glory
of God is its light, and its lamp is the Lamb" (Rev 21:23).
We shall come at last to him who is the true Light, and who
is our life.

The Psalms are the songs of pilgrims who make their way
towards the heavenly Jerusalem; they are the songs of those
who work in the field of the Lord, those who go out weeping, bearing the seed for sowing, but come back singing for
joy, carrying their sheaves: by their beauty, they entice us
to long for the fulfilment of God's promises. I have spoken
frequently of the fact that we do not yet see this fulfilment,
that we have not yet been made one with God. But here, indeed, we do have a taste of what that unity will be like: in
our earthly worship, we take part in the eternal liturgy of
heaven, concelebrating with the angels (as the eastern tradition expresses it). We live still in the period of the fragmentary — but however fitful our vision of the glory that one
day will be revealed, it is a *real* vision we have. We do

indeed see as in a mirror, dimly — but still, we see! The words which Christ speaks to us may not be altogether clear to us — but still, he does speak to us. He has not left us to wander aimlessly, but has given us his company on our journey. Just as the two disciples on the road to Emmaus on Easter Day did not recognise their travelling companion, so we often fail to recognise Christ in our midst. But always he is there, calling to us, "Arise, my love, my fair one, and come away!" (Song 2:13). Always, he is waiting eagerly for our response.

You will have noticed that I have often quoted the Song of Songs in these meditations. This book is the poetry *par excellence* of the love of Christ and ourselves, a poetry that is bold enough to put into words the things we experience but scarcely dare to name: our longing for Christ and his longing for us, our terror when we call and do not find him, and the profound tranquillity of the union into which he invites us — "I am my beloved's and my beloved is mine; he pastures his flock among the lilies" (6:3). Rabbi Aqiba, who died in A.D. 135, replied to another Jewish leader who said that the Song of Songs was not part of scripture, "All the ages are not worth the day on which the Song of Songs was given to Israel. For all the writings are holy, but the Song of Songs is the holy of holies."

The Holy of Holies, we may remember, is a place to be entered with dread — not a place to be rushed into carelessly. We must first be purified before we can be united in the sort of love of which the Song of Songs speaks; that is the universal teaching of the mystics of the Church's tradition. Part of the purpose of our prayer of the Psalms, as we have reflected, is to accomplish in us that purification, that transfiguration of our whole being by the light of God. But part also of the purpose of our prayer of the Psalms is actually to celebrate that union in love which we experience even now, even though in us the process of cleansing has not yet been completed. For the Lord does not wait until we have passed the examination, so to speak, before he gives us the prizes: even while we are still learning, still pupils in his school, he shows us what our final reward will be. He does not withhold himself from us if we seek him: he is close to all who call on his name, and, even in the midst of our sinfulness, he is present, summoning us to open our hearts to him, to permit him to enter and purify us.

Psalm 121 is one of the Psalms that remind us of our need for purification, but it also reminds us that even now God is with us. It is a song of joy, of delight in the presence of the Lord, like the joy of the bride in the Song of Songs: "With great delight I sat in his shadow, and his fruit was sweet to my taste. He brought me to the banqueting house, and his banner over me was love" (2:3-4). So here, the psalmist cries out, "I rejoiced!" He is not like a child who objects to being pushed out to church on a Sunday morning: no, he runs to be with the Lord whom he loves, to enter his holy place. "And now our feet are standing within your gates, O Jerusalem!"

Jerusalem is "built as a city, which is bound firmly together", a place of peace, a community strengthened by the presence of the gifts of the Holy Spirit, "love, joy, peace, patience, kindness, goodness", and all the other things St Paul lists (cf. Gal 5:22-23). All these are indeed present in the Church, and so she can give praise to her maker: "It is there that the tribes go up, the tribes of the Lord. For Israel's law it is, there to praise the Lord's name." And yet, we remain a community of sinners, and so we must pray for forgiveness. The Jerusalem which is bound firmly together in peace is a city which only the righteous can enter, as we are told in the Book of Revelation (21:8, 27): "There were set the thrones of judgement of the house of David", says our psalm. Once again, if we affirm that the Church is holy, as we do every Sunday at Mass in the creed, then we commit ourselves to the judgement of the Lord, we commit ourselves to becoming holy. And since we recognise his presence within us, we can truly give him thanks.

The second part of this psalm is a prayer for Jerusalem, a prayer that reminds us urgently that no one in the Church is ever so holy that we can forget to pray for them. All the peace and joy of the Church's fellowship come from the Lord, not from us — as for you and me, we are constantly a threat to the unity which nourishes us. And so we say, "May peace reign in your walls, in your palaces, peace! For love of my brethren and friends I say: 'Peace upon you!'" We cannot ever escape our duty to pray. Even in the depth of our union of love, we cannot forget that this is a precarious union which our sinfulness constantly threatens.

For the disciple, there are no shortcuts, as we have seen. There is no resurrection without the cross, for, as Jesus says (in one of the sayings preserved, not in the New Testament, but in the second-century Gospel of Thomas), "He who is near *me* is near the *fire*." The fire is something frightening; but, even more frightening, for those who have begun to taste his sweetness, is the second part of that saying — "But he who is far from *me* is far from the *kingdom*." "Taste and see that the Lord is good", invites the psalmist (33:8). When once we have tasted, when once we have heard his voice, when once we have seen his face, then no suffering, no fire, can utterly terrify us. For he tells us, "I have overcome the world" (Jn 16:33), and if that is so, then nothing in this world can ultimately hold us back from his love.

And so, let us pray . . .